Design Thinking

This design focused series publishes books aimed at helping Designers, Design Researchers, Developers, and Storytellers understand what's happening on the leading edge of creativity. Today's designers are being asked to invent new paradigms and approaches every day – they need the freshest thinking and techniques. This series challenges creative minds to design bigger.

More information about this series at https://www.springer.com/series/15933

Coding Art

The Four Steps to Creative Programming with the Processing Language

Yu Zhang
Mathias Funk

Apress®

Coding Art: The Four Steps to Creative Programming with the Processing Language

Yu Zhang
Eindhoven, The Netherlands

Mathias Funk
Eindhoven, The Netherlands

ISBN-13 (pbk): 978-1-4842-6263-4
https://doi.org/10.1007/978-1-4842-6264-1

ISBN-13 (electronic): 978-1-4842-6264-1

Managing Director, Apress Media LLC: Welmoed Spahr
Acquisitions Editor: Natalie Pao
Development Editor: James Markham
Coordinating Editor: Jessica Vakili

Distributed to the book trade worldwide by Springer Science+Business Media New York, 1 NY Plaza, New York, NY 10004. Phone 1-800-SPRINGER, fax (201) 348-4505, e-mail orders-ny@springer-sbm.com, or visit www.springeronline.com. Apress Media, LLC is a California LLC and the sole member (owner) is Springer Science + Business Media Finance Inc (SSBM Finance Inc). SSBM Finance Inc is a **Delaware** corporation.

For information on translations, please e-mail booktranslations@springernature.com; for reprint, paperback, or audio rights, please e-mail bookpermissions@springernature.com.

Apress titles may be purchased in bulk for academic, corporate, or promotional use. eBook versions and licenses are also available for most titles. For more information, reference our Print and eBook Bulk Sales web page at http://www.apress.com/bulk-sales.

Any source code or other supplementary material referenced by the author in this book is available to readers on GitHub via the book's product page, located at www.apress.com/978-1-4842-6263-4. For more detailed information, please visit http://www.apress.com/source-code.

Printed on acid-free paper

Table of Contents

About the Authors

An artist by training, **Yu Zhang** finished her PhD in 2017 on the theory and artistic practice of interactive technologies for public, large-scale installations. She approaches visual art with mixed reality installations and projections, sensor-based interactives, and computational arts. She roots her artistic intent in the symbolism of Asian traditions and transforms the artistic unpacking of drama and cultural signifiers into experiences of interactivity and connectivity that ultimately bridge artistic expression and audience experience. She uses systems design toolkit, to realize a complex multifaceted experience playing with the spatiotemporal context of the audience's interaction with the installations when digital and physical converge. Starting from interactivity, she constructs layers of different connections between artist, artwork, audience, and the environment to express how far such connectivity can impact and reshape the structure and relations of objects, space, and time within a dynamic audience experience. Apart from her artistic research and practice, Yu's teaching experiences cover over ten years and a broad space including traditional classrooms and design-led project-based learning activities.

Mathias Funk is Associate Professor in the Future Everyday group in the Department of Industrial Design at the Eindhoven University of Technology (TU/e). He has a background in Computer Science and a PhD in Electrical Engineering (from Eindhoven University of Technology). His research interests include complex systems design, remote data collection, systems for musical expression, and design tools such as domain-specific languages and integrated development environments. In the past, he has worked in research positions at ATR Japan, RWTH Aachen, and he has been Visiting Researcher at Philips Consumer Lifestyle, the Netherlands. He is also the co-founder of UXsuite, a high-tech spin-off from Eindhoven University of Technology. He has years of experience in software architecture and design, engineering of distributed systems, and web technologies. Further areas of interest and practice are domain-specific languages and code generation, sound and video processing systems, and data and information visualization approaches. He has been involved extensively in the business side of innovation, the transfer of research to commercial products, and he loves to think about a design's real-world impact. As a teacher, he teaches various technology-oriented courses in the Industrial Design curriculum about designing with data and visualization approaches, systems design, and technologies for connected products and systems. He is regularly invited to give international workshops on large-scale interactive systems, group music improvisation interfaces, and expressive (musical) interaction. He has been an active musician for years and is very interested in the intersection of music, art, and design in particular.

About the Technical Reviewer

Bin Yu received his MS in biomedical engineering from Northeastern University, Shenyang, China, in 2012, and his PhD in industrial design from the Eindhoven University of Technology, in 2018. He is currently a Data Designer at Philips Design, the Netherlands, and specializes in both human–computer interaction and data visualization.

Acknowledgments

We started this book in October 2018 and went through the process of writing for several months, ending with an intensive summer writing retreat at Tenjinyama Art Studio in Sapporo. We are grateful for the hospitality and kindness of Mami Odai and her team, and we will always remember these weeks on the hill with the wind rushing through the dark trees.

From October 2019, we sent out the manuscript to reviewers, and we would like to acknowledge their hard work and sincerely thank them for great feedback and suggestions, warm-hearted encouragement, and praise: Loe Feijs (Eindhoven University of Technology), Jia Han (Sony Shanghai Creative Center), Garyfalia Pitsaki (3quarters.design), Bart Hengeveld (Eindhoven University of Technology), Joep Elderman (BMD Studio), Ansgar Silies (independent artist), and Rung-Huei Liang (National Taiwan University of Science and Technology). Without you, the book would not have been as clear and rich. We also thank the great team at Apress, Natalie and Jessica, and especially Bin Yu for his excellent technical review. Finally, we deeply appreciate the support from friends and family for this project.

CHAPTER 1

Introduction

The art world is interwoven with technology and actually quite innovative and playful. From cave paintings to the use of perspective, novel colors, and lighting, to printing techniques and direct inclusion of machines and code, there are examples of how art broke ground and changed its shape forever. Already before the beginning of the twenty-first century, artists used code and programmed machines to generate art or even be part of it.

There are so many examples of technology in art. It is also interesting to see the path of how it has grown in the past 70 years. Famous examples are, for instance, of earlier pioneers in Computer Art like Georg Nees, Michael Noll, Vera Molnár, and Frieder Nake who brought the use of pseudo-randomness and algorithm about fractals and recursion in code drawing. The young generation of artists like Casey Reas, who is well-known for developing the Processing software, extend artistic ideas through the programming language. Some artists like Jared Tarbell introduce real data into art creation and connect the complexity with the data availability. It is remarkable that for most of their works, computer artists open the source code to the public, so we can learn from them.

In this book, we want to make the point that the use of modern technology and machines in creative work does not contradict "creative expression." Instead, if used well, technology can help creatives take steps in new directions, think of new ideas, and ultimately discover their ideal form of expression.

© Yu Zhang, Mathias Funk 2021
Y. Zhang and M. Funk, *Coding Art*, https://doi.org/10.1007/978-1-4842-6264-1_1

CHAPTER 1   INTRODUCTION

Why data and information in art? The use of data can connect artworks to the human body, signals from outer space, or contemporary societal issues, important events happening all over the world. With data streams, creative works can become "alive." As they represent data in visual or auditory forms, they comment on what is happening in the world; they provide an alternative frame to news and noteworthy. They can react and even create their own data as a response.

Why is interaction interesting for creatives? Interaction in an artwork opens a channel for communication with individual viewers or an entire audience. Interaction can make a work more immersive and let viewers engage in new ways with the artist's ideas. Some might want to engage with art emotionally; some others prefer a more rational approach. The creative is in charge of defining and also limiting interactivity – from fully open access to careful limitations that preserve the overall aesthetics and message of the work. Interaction can help create multifaceted artworks that show different views on the world, or even allow for exploration of unknown territory.

Using computation and code can help a creative express ideas independent of medium and channel – the work is foremost conceptual and can be rendered in any form susceptible to the viewer. So, when we express an artistic concept in the form of code or machine instructions, we can direct the machine to produce its output in a number of ways: print a rendered image on a postcard or t-shirt, project an animation onto a building, or make an expressive interaction accessible from a single screen or for a global audience on the Internet. By disconnecting from physical matter, we create ephemeral art that might even change hands and be changed by others.

Ultimately, technology transforms what it is applied to. We show you how to do this with creativity.

1.1 Coding art

What is "coding art" all about? The title is intentionally ambiguous, ranging in meaning from how to code art to coding as creative expression. Probably the message that resonates most with you is somewhere in the middle.

Tips   We are curious what you think during or after reading and working with this book. Please let us know on our website.[1]

In this book, "coding" simply means an action that translates meaning from one language into another, for example, from natural language into a computer language. This translation, as any translation, implies a change in who can and will interpret what we express in the new language. It also implies thinking about how this interpretation might work out toward a result. For natural languages, we empathize with other people, how they think and act. For machines, we need something called "computational thinking" [3, 6, 21].

Learning how to code is quite similar to learning how to speak another language. Some people might follow a more theoretical approach and learn vocabulary and grammar before attempting to speak and converse. Some others start with a conversation and gradually understand the structure of the language behind it. Depending on the circumstances, any approach might work well.

For teaching how to code in a computer or programming language, both approaches have been used in the past. There are very theoretical ways to approach coding. They often come with a steep learning curve and the full richness of what the language creators intend you to know about it. And there are also ways to playfully get used to simple examples that teach

---

[1]https://codingart-book.com/feedback

3

the basics before moving to more complicated examples. In the context of creative work, we strongly feel that the second approach, starting with the "conversation," works far better. However, we have seen in practice that the playful approach often hits a limitation: how to make the step from toy examples to something that is useful and also complex and intricate. This is hard and the reason why we write this book.

1.2 Motivation

Every profession, every vocation, is about doing something difficult with high quality, often using specific approaches or techniques. This works for engineers, researchers, marketing, and doing business. For creatives, the "difficult thing" is the invention of meaning and purpose out of a large set of options, constraints, and relations. It is a very human thing to create, which means we apply both our intuition and our training and knowledge to a challenge. Creatives apply various technologies in a creative process, and coding is a part of that. In this book, the use of coding in creative work is based on the situation that we try to construct meaning through understanding the logic and structure of coding. We use coding as a creative tool rather than being hardcore programmers or mere end users.

1.2.1 How to talk with a "machine"

Confronted with the particular but different characteristics of art, design, and technology, we have seen creatives struggle with questions about "how to start," "how to continue," and "how to end" while working with code and coding practice. Like writing a book or essay, it is difficult to code an idea in an individual context and condition, so that a machine can produce something meaningful for us. Unlike writing, the machine will respond swiftly to anything we feed it. It will never complain about too much work and always accurately reflect what we write in coded language.

And when we get things wrong, make a mistake, which happens more often than we are comfortable with, then this is on us. The machine is a "stupid" thing, dull and rational. Whatever creativity emerges is ours only. This book is essentially about how to let the machine express and amplify our human creativity by using precise instructions ("code") and input ("data").

For many creatives, the use of code in their projects brings new challenges, beyond successfully completing a project. For example, an unforeseen challenge is to let the work operate reliably for hours, days, and weeks. With traditional "static" material, creative output eventually turns into a stable form that rests in itself. Paper, photo, clay, concrete, metal, video, or audio documentary are stable. There are established ways to keep them safe and maintain their quality. If you want, you can study this conservation craft as a university subject even.

Things are different for art or design based on code. Code always needs a machine to run on, an environment to perform its function. This essentially counteracts technological progress: there is always a newer machine, a more modern operating system, a more powerful way to program something. Any of these get in and code written for earlier machines may stop working. This does not happen that easily to a painting or a designed and manufactured object.

1.2.2 Practice a practice

When we write about "coding" as a practice, we try to combine the creative process with computational thinking. Over the years, our art or design students, inevitably, encounter similar problems. They often ask questions like "why do we need to learn coding?", "coding is so difficult to continue once you are stuck, what is it worth?", and "I could understand the examples (from the programming software references) well, but I cannot do my idea just by using those examples, how to do that?". These questions (or often passionate complaints) point at the difficulty of learning coding as a new language. It seems that there is a big disconnect of "brainy" coding from creative practice. There is a common understanding that creative expression is fueled by inspiration and directed by intuition. In contrast, "coding" or working with technology seems to be very rational and thought through. Yes, nice try. Creative coding is only slightly "brainy" at the beginning. Soon after, it will turn into something intuitively creative and much faster than learning to wield a brush and master the skills to paint.

1.2.3 Do it and own it

Before we can start, here is yet another big "why" question: even if coding is an indispensable part of a creative project, why do artists or designers need to do the code themselves? Cooperative skills are basic for any contemporary artist and designer. Although there are cases of successful international artists who command a multidisciplinary team to work on their ideas, these people are absolutely not the norm. More realistically, we see creatives who cannot afford a team of qualified experts and who work on smaller budgets and projects. Our point in this book is: without understanding coding and technology to some extent, it will be very difficult to work with experts productively or get help when you run into problems. The point about creative technology is: you want something? Then do it and own it.

We are aware that creatives who are learning or exploring interactive art, digital art, and new media art are no longer just following one traditional approach. Instead, they need to work with their ideas from a broader perspective – in the principles of science, technology, engineering, and mathematics (STEM). When we move into the field where art meets code, creatives may need a new way of thinking and working which can help them see this new field through the lens of an old field where they have been active in and professional at.

In projects where code is involved, you as the creative need the ability to read code, understand code, perhaps even write code, and think in a computational structure. This is necessary for effectively communicating with technology experts in a common "language." We think these are essential abilities creatives today need to have. Besides, creatives who rely mostly on the help of experts often feel uncertain as to how much control they have to relinquish to achieve the goal. We actually have a section on working with technology experts towards the end of the book.

1.3 How to read this book

This book can be read in different ways, from different perspectives and also with different pre-knowledge and backgrounds. It is hard to find a common ground, but we hope that with patience and openness, you will soon see our point.

1.3.1 Calling all creatives

First of all, this book is dedicated to creatives who might be designers, artists, design or art students. We also wrote this book for architects, engineers, and researchers. They all share that creativity makes their profession special and their work unique. The creative will benefit mostly by taking the main road from beginning to end, visiting all examples and typing along. Why not bring this book to your favorite café once a week and slowly make your way through the different chapters. If you space it out over several weeks, you will see that the breaks will spark new thoughts of how to code art and what you could do yourself with the current week's topic.

We also wrote this book for educators who could take a jump to the last part first. There we explain more about the rationale behind the concepts we introduce and our methodology. We show how everything fits together, also from an educational point of view.

Third, this book is written for technical experts, who know it all actually and who might be surprised by the simplicity of the code examples. Why would they read this book? Because they realize that knowing code as a second native language and being able to construct the architecture of code is not enough, by far. The embedding of code in a process, driven by creativity or business interests, is where the challenges lie. As a technical expert, you will find the third part most interesting and can use it as a lens to scan the first two parts.

1.3.2 Four steps, one example, one zoom

In the first main part of this book, we will go through a creative process in four steps and explain how coding works in each step. The steps will each unfold through several practical examples and conclude with a short summary.

The first step, idea to visuals, gives you a short primer into working with Processing and the different visual elements that are readily available to you. We quickly proceed to working with the visual canvas before diving into animation and interaction. From this point onward, you know how to draw moving things on a canvas that might even respond to your interactive control. The second step is about composition and structure, that is, how we let art emerge from a multitude of different elements on the canvas. We will introduce data and code structure that help you in working with many visual elements at the same time. Together, we apply this in several examples around visual structure. In the third step, we show you how to work things out in more detail and how to give depth to your creations. You will learn about randomness and noise and how to control them artistically. We show you how to create smooth animations and transitions between different elements and colors. Interactivity returns in this step, and we show you how to combine interactive input with composition and refinement. The fourth step is about production, how to bring your creation to the stage, how to produce and present it well in different media from high-resolution printing to interactive installations.

On the next page, we show an example that we created inspired by an abstract geometrical painting of Kazimir Malevich ("Suprematisme," 1915) as inspiration (Figure 1-1). We chose this work because, for us, it visually hinted at a very interesting motion of otherwise static blocks that seems to be captured in a moment just before toppling over. We started with a recreation of the visual composition of ten basic elements in similar primary colors on a cream-colored canvas (step 1). In a second step, we connected to the impression of inherent motion and work with the blocks: we shifted and redrew the same composition recursively, adding more and more layers over time (step 2). The third step involved adding three large-scale rotated copies of the composition to complete the circular perspective. We also fine-tuned the timing of adding the different elements and operations over time, so the work developed in a few minutes from the first screen and visually stabilized in the last screen. Finally, we added a gradual shift of the entire canvas that, over several minutes, zoomed out and shifted the center of the canvas from the left top to the right bottom (step 3). In the fourth step, we "produce" the images that you see: we let the animation play and live select tens of frames to be automatically rendered. From these frames, we finally select eight frames as they exhibit good composition individually and also show the motion of the entire work well (step 4).

This example shows how we borrow from the four large steps described in this book, by picking a few pieces from each step that match our concept. From a process point of view, steps 1, 3, and 4 were relatively straightforward. We took more time for the second step because we went into two different directions, one more playful and one more technical, of which the playful was the right one at the end after trying both. Only after resolving this, we could move faster again. There are chances that you will struggle as well while working with this book; don't forget to take breaks and never let go.

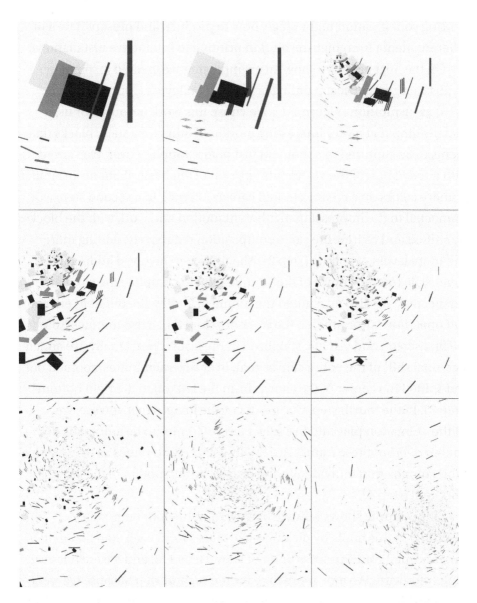

Figure 1-1. *Example of generative art taking an abstract geometrical painting of Kazimir Malevich ("Suprematisme," 1915) as inspiration*

Throughout these four steps, we will teach you about creative computation, and, at some point, you will see also bits of strategies, patterns, and more complex concepts appear. Afterward, we will roll up all steps in a larger art project, MOUNTROTHKO, in the second part of this book. Finally, in the third part, we zoom out and turn toward the practice of creative coding, through learning and collaboration. This part shows you how you can make progress using this book and beyond, what you can do when you feel stuck, and how to get help. It's all there, you just need to go step by step toward it.

1.3.3 Getting ready

This book contains a lot of examples, and they are written in code ("source code"). Most examples can be used directly, and the resulting visual output is shown close to the source code.

Code examples

```
// How to quickly find code examples in the book?
```

Look for text in a box like this!

All source code listed in this book is written in the open source software Processing. Processing itself is available from `https://processing.org`, and we recommend that you install it on your computer to get the most out of this book. Processing is a medium for understanding the structure and logic of code. We will explain this shortly. The code examples are available online from our Processing library.[2]

---

[2]The Processing library can be found here: `https://codingart-book.com/library`. You can install it using the Processing library manager.

Although it might be tempting to just download the examples and play with them, we recommend typing them yourself (at least some of them). This way, you will pick up the programming style much faster and allow your muscle memory to support your learning. And if you are lucky, you will make a few small mistakes that give you surprising results.

Finally, we will address you, the reader, informally. Think of this book as a conversation in your favorite café over coffee and your laptop is right in front of you. Feel free to pause the conversation and dive into a topic on your own, or explore the code of the examples, and then resume to the next page. Let's begin.

PART I

Creative coding

CHAPTER 2

Idea to visuals

In this first part of the book, we will go through four process steps and show for each step how coding becomes a meaningful part of our creative process. In step 1, IDEA TO VISUALS, we take a bottom-up approach and start directly with visuals and code. Our entry point to this approach is to use code directly from the ideation stage of the creative process. More specifically, instead of making mood boards, sketching, writing, searching the web, or talking to experts, we suggest that you just start Processing and give it a spin. First, we look at how we can express our ideas using Processing and a few lines of code. Yes, we start really simple.

2.1 Visual elements

For many artists, even if visual elements in their work are coded, the standards for effectiveness in their work are still based on either cognitive or aesthetic goals [12, 18, 20]. When we analyze any drawings, paintings, sculptures, or designs, it is similar – we examine and decompose them to see how they are put together to create the overall effect of the work. Lines, colors, shapes, scale, form, and textures are the general fundamental components of aesthetics and cognition for both art and design and for coding art as well.

Processing can draw a wide range of different forms that result from variation and combination of simple shapes. When you take an example from the Processing reference, try to change the numbers in the example to explore how the shape changes and responds to different numbers.

© Yu Zhang, Mathias Funk 2021
Y. Zhang and M. Funk, *Coding Art*, https://doi.org/10.1007/978-1-4842-6264-1_2

The first two examples show that you can hit play in Processing as often as you want and see how your work is evolving over time. Sometimes, it is good to look at the results, just after changing a single value. By moving fast between the code and the canvas, you will also learn faster and get a better understanding of how the code influences the drawing of shapes and how you can control precisely what is drawn on the canvas. At the same time, by going through two detailed examples, we want to give you a feeling for how important the Processing reference is as well.

We recommend having a browser window open with the Processing reference web page, so you can quickly jump into an explanation without losing momentum in creating with Processing. First shapes coming up, you have Processing started up and ready?

2.1.1 Shapes

Every visual element in Processing follows one of two patterns: (1) first specifying position, then size, and then shape or (2) specifying the points on which the shape is drawn. We will come back to this in a few pages. By carefully looking through these examples about simple visual elements, you will understand the similarities in the code for ellipse and rectangle and also the similarities for line, point, curve, polygon, and triangle.

Let's start with a simple example based on the "ellipse" shape. Open Processing and type in the following three lines of code to draw a simple circle:

First drawing: a simple ellipse with a black border

```
// Draw a simple ellipse
noFill();
stroke(0, 0, 0);
ellipse(56, 46, 55, 55);

// Try copying and pasting the code several times
// with different values to create layered shapes.
```

In this example, we draw an ellipse with equal width and height, so we get a perfect circle. Processing usually fills shapes white with a black border. This standard behavior can be changed, for instance, by using the noFill function in our example.

Reminder   Correct spelling is really important in programming. So, you need to carefully check that it is noFill and not nofill, for example.

When going through the code, you notice something interesting: the spelling of Processing functions like noFill is quite special; it starts with a lowercase character, and then there is an uppercase character in the middle. This is a naming convention for several programming languages that allows to distinguish different words that are combined in a function name. This combination is necessary because Processing cannot deal with spaces inside a name, and still we want to be able to read and understand the function name. The solution is to combine the words and use uppercase characters at the beginning of every word inside the combination of words – all except the first one. Processing checks this before running any program, and it will "complain" if the spelling is wrong. Try spelling a few things wrong in the preceding program, and see how Processing reacts. This will be helpful in the future.

Back to our example: The circle is not filled, but we still draw a thin line around the circle. The width of the line is set to 1 pixel automatically. We can change the color of the line with the stroke function. We use three numbers to specify the amounts of red, green, and blue in the color. The amounts range from 0 to 255.

? Think about this

Try playing with different values for the different color components. Can you create a deep purple color or a light beige just by using different color values?

This is also known as the RGB color mode. Here, we just use the RGB values of black color (0, 0, 0). If we would increase the three values from 0 to 120 each, we would see a gray color, and if we turn them all up to 255, the resulting color is white.

If we look at the last line of the code example, the first two numbers, 56 and 46, give us the location of the element. When positioning an element on the digital canvas, the first number always refers to the horizontal position or x coordinate. The second number refers to the vertical position or y coordinate. That's why they are usually called x and y. We refer to a point or position on the canvas as (x, y), in our example, (56, 46). Our ellipse is drawn as a circle with equal width and height which are both 55. Now, try changing the values in ellipse to see different shapes of the ellipse and in stroke which will give the ellipse outline a different color. Can you stretch the ellipse sideways or turn the outline green?

After the first ellipse example, the next example shows how we can change a few numbers and see a very different drawing of the circle.

There is also a new element of code: the code comment. Code comments allow us to leave thoughts and ideas in the middle of the code that help us understand it at a later moment or help communicate the main ideas to others. Code comments start with double slashes // and will be rendered gray in Processing. This means that Processing knows these are just comments and will ignore them when drawing.

Draw a centered and filled ellipse on a purple background

```
// set the size of the canvas
size(600, 600);

// first, paint the background purple
background(208, 170, 208);

// set line color and width and fill color
stroke(246, 173, 113);
strokeWeight(10);
fill(113, 70, 132);

// draw the ellipse in center of canvas
ellipse(width/2, height/2, 320, 320);
```

In this example, we first set the size of the canvas with the size function. The first number is the width and the second number the height of the digital canvas (Figure 2-1). In this case, both width and height of the canvas are 640. We will use the width and height later in the example, when drawing the ellipse. Another new thing in this example is the background color of the digital canvas, which is defined according to RGB (208, 170, 208) color using the background function. In addition to just defining stroke color, we also define the width of the stroke (strokeWeight) and the RGB color that is used to fill the drawn elements. In this example, the position of the ellipse, that is, the x and y coordinates, is located in the center of the digital canvas. We achieve this by replacing the first two numbers by the width and height of the canvas, each divided by 2. When we divide the width by 2, we effectively get the horizontal middle point and same for the height. Now, we can use these two new values to position the ellipse and draw it in size 320 by 320 pixels.

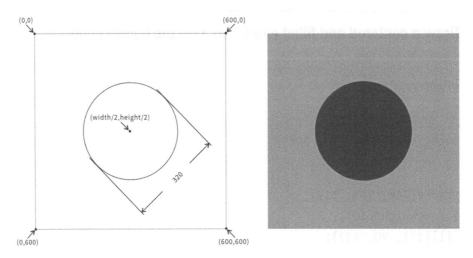

Figure 2-1. *Canvas measurements (left) and drawn circle (right). The canvas measures 600 pixels in width and height*

In the following part of this section, we will look at the visual elements in general and quickly show the code example of using such elements in Processing environment.

2.1.2 Shaping up in Processing

The line as a visual element is really everywhere in art and design. Processing draws lines as a path between two points on the digital canvas.

Draw a simple line

```
// draw line from position (21, 22) to position (31, 32)
line(21, 22, 31, 32);
```

In the Processing environment, the line also could be imagined as a dynamic path in which a tiny dot is moving between two defined positions on the canvas – or simply as the tip of a pencil or brush moving from the first point to the second point in a straight line.

A second shape in Processing that is drawn by points is the `triangle`. Here, we specify three different points as pairs of coordinates. Unlike the line, the triangle can be filled, so we should also think about using `fill` before. Why before? Because Processing really does things step by step: first, prepare how to draw a shape, then draw it, and then the next. If we draw two shapes and the second should look different than the first, then we first draw the first shape, change the looks, and then draw the second shape. And if we don't change the looks, then Processing will just keep the previous settings.

? Think about this

Can you guess what this triangle will look like? Try it out in Processing to see if you are right.

Draw a triangle

```
fill(140, 40, 160);

// draw triangle between position (21, 22),
// position (31, 32), and position (41, 22)
triangle(21, 22, 31, 32, 41, 22);
```

Processing offers more shapes that are just defined by points, for examples, quad (four points) or even complex polygons that are freely defined by a list of multiple points. You can check the Processing reference how to use them.

21

We have seen another shape in Processing that was defined not by different points, but by giving a position and then the size of the shape. The first example is the ellipse function, which allows to draw circles and ellipses. Another shape is the rect function that allows to draw squares and rectangles on the canvas.

Draw a rectangle

```
fill(140, 180, 20);

// draw rectangle at position (21, 22) with
// size given by width 70 and height 30
rect(21, 22, 70, 30);
```

We can draw the same rectangle with rounded corners by adding a fifth value to the rect function: the corner radius.

Draw a rectangle with rounded corners

```
// the last argument is the corner radius
rect(21, 22, 70, 30, 10);
```

In this example, the top-left corner of the rectangle is in position (21, 22), because Processing positions visual elements by default with their top-left corner. Processing can interpret the position of a shape in different ways. There is the CORNER mode that takes the position as the top-left corner, and there is the CENTER mode that takes the position as the center of the shape. Both can be useful in different situations. Let's see how it works for drawing rectangles.

Draw two rounded rectangles with different positioning

```
// draw rounded rectangle with (21, 22) as center
rectMode(CENTER);
fill(255, 0, 0);
rect(21, 22, 70, 30, 10);

// draw rounded rectangle with (21, 22) as top-left corner
rectMode(CORNER);
fill(0, 0, 255);
rect(21, 22, 70, 30, 10);
```

The first rectangle is drawn with rectMode(CENTER), which means that the position parameters (first and second parameters) are interpreted as the center point of the rectangle. As a result, the rectangle is drawn around this center point. The second rectangle in the preceding example is drawn with the rectMode(CORNER), which changes the location interpretation to the upper-left corner. As a result, the rectangle has its upper-left corner at the given position (first and second parameter) and then extends right and down by width and height, respectively.

Tips   You don't have to repeat the rectMode function. It applies to all rectangles until you call rectMode again with a different setting.

2.1.3 Colors, transparency, and filters

Artists play with color through different art mediums – acrylic, oil color, watercolor, ink, colored pencils, or mixed materials. Each of these mediums has its own characteristics, and each requires its specific techniques for using in art practice.

23

Whenever we want to use color in Processing functions such as `fill`, `stroke`, `background`, and many others, we specify the color by its channels: red, green, and blue in the RGB mode and hue, saturation, and brightness in the HSB mode. Two different color modes can be used in Processing: RGB or HSB. If there is no `colorMode` specified in the code, then the default of RGB with scale of 0–255 is used.

When we use three values to specify the red, green, and blue channels of a color, we notice that for grayscale colors from black (0, 0, 0) to white (255, 255, 255), the three values are the same. In this case, we can just use a single value, and Processing will understand that we want to use the same value for all three channels.

Shortcut to draw grayscale colors

```
// lightgray
fill(180, 180, 180);

// same lightgray
fill(180);
```

With multiple shapes that overlap, we might want to work with transparency in our canvas drawing. That is very easy in Processing: just add the `alpha` transparency as the fourth value in any function that specifies color, for example, `fill` or `stroke`.

Fill colors with transparency

```
// solid purple
fill(180, 0, 180);

// 50% transparent purple (255 * 0.5 = 128)
fill(180, 0, 180, 128);
```

In addition to using colors and transparency, there are also several filters which can be applied to achieve special color effects, for example, filter(GRAY) (turn colors into grayscale), filter(INVERT) (invert the colors), filter(POSTERIZE) (reduce the number of colors), or filter(BLUR) (blur the image). By giving different values to these filters, they produce striking creative effects.

The following piece of code is based on the line and color functions in Processing to draw an image which contains a variety of color and line combinations (Figure 2-2). This image is inspired by the Dutch artist Piet Mondrian and his 1942 painting "New York City I" [15]. To achieve the effect in the image, arranging the order of lines in the code might be the part that needs the most patience. Why? Processing runs the code line by line. The first lines in the code will be drawn first, and the following lines will be drawn on top of them, thereby creating layers of digital paint. What you see on top is drawn last.

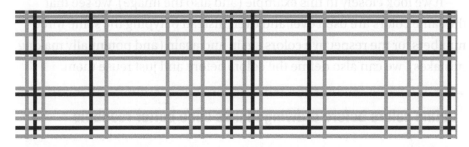

Figure 2-2. *Reproduction of a Mondrian painting "New York City I"*

Draw lines in different colors and orientations

```
// set canvas size, white background
size(1920, 1080);
background(255);
// set 30 pixel line weight
strokeWeight(30);
```

```
// set color and draw line
stroke (9, 37, 87);
line (0, 980, width, 980);
stroke (135, 3, 17);
line (0, 10, width, 10);

stroke (9, 37, 87);
line (0, 90, width, 90);

stroke (211, 179, 15);
line (100, 0, 100, height);

stroke (211, 179, 15);
line (0, 650, width, 650);

// many more lines ...
```

If we look closely in this example (and also the image), we see that the same colors are used over and over. Instead of typing the same three numbers for the respective colors again and again (and potentially making mistakes), we can also define the colors before and just reuse them.

Define colors before drawing makes code better readable

```
// define blue, red and yellow
color blue = color(9, 37, 87);
color red = color(135, 3, 17);
color yellow = color(211, 179, 15);

// set colors and draw line
stroke (blue);
line (0, 980, width, 980);
stroke (red);
line (0, 10, width, 10);
```

```
stroke (blue);
line (0, 90, width, 90);
stroke (yellow);
line (100, 0, 100, height);
stroke (yellow);
line (0, 650, width, 650);

// many more lines ...
```

We define three variables blue, red, and yellow. They will "hold" the three different colors, and we can always refer to them when using stroke. This is a first example of how we can structure our code to make it better readable. We will come back to this later when looking at the overall structure of code.

2.1.4 Working with form and texture

When we compare Processing to powerful graphic software like SketchUp, 3DS Max, Cinema 4D, or Unity which focus on modeling parametric and organic structures and rendering a surface's texture in a variety of styles, we see that Processing seems very simple, almost too simple. The interface has just a few buttons and menus, and there is a large empty text area for code. In fact, Processing allows to do similar things as the preceding applications; it simply exposes the functionality in a different way. Some things are harder to achieve in Processing, but there are also things that would be difficult in the applications mentioned earlier. If you want to try these features, give the application a try and then import the created forms and textures into Processing. It is sometimes easier to achieve the desired result by using the strengths of different software packages instead of trying to do everything in one application.

"As one of basic visual elements in Arts, form encloses volume, having length, width, and height. A form is a shape in three dimensions, versus shape, which is two-dimensional, or flat" [14]. In Processing, if we draw a 3D object, the object must be drawn on a canvas that is created with the P3D parameter at the end (see next example). This means that the canvas is prepared to render all elements in 3D. When drawing in a 3D canvas, we also need to be more aware that the viewer position, the "camera," matters.

The 3D objects are interesting starting points for artistic ideas. The following example is based on the code of drawing a simple ellipse in Processing environment from the beginning of this section. We keep most values the same and only change the type of canvas with P3D to show the difference between 2D and 3D shape. We also change the shape of the ellipse into a 3D form: a sphere (Figure 2-3).

? Think about this

Moving from 2D to 3D is not difficult in Processing. We suggest that you look at the two code examples in parallel to see the difference in drawing 2D and 3D objects.

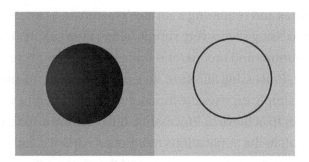

Figure 2-3. *3D sphere (left, drawn with sphere) and 2D circle (right, draw with ellipse)*

Draw on a 3D canvas with directional light

```
// set canvas size and ask for 3D canvas
size(640, 640, P3D);
background(208, 170, 208);
noStroke();
fill(113, 70, 132);

// use a directional light in 3D space:
// first three values give the light position,
// the rest is about the direction of the light
directionalLight(255, 220, 255, 1, 0, -1);

// move camera
translate(width/2, height/2, -30);

// draw sphere with 180 pixel diameter
sphere(180);
```

Processing offers more shapes and even more lighting and material properties. Again, check the Processing reference for inspiration.

One important property of 3D forms is texture. "At its most basic, texture is defined as a tactile quality of an object's surface. It appeals to our sense of touch, which can evoke feelings of pleasure, discomfort, or familiarity. Artists use this knowledge to elicit emotional responses from people who view their work. The reasons for doing so vary greatly, but texture is a fundamental element in many pieces of art"[8]. In the following, we will go into one simple example of adding a texture to a sphere. We first use loadImage to load an image for the texture which is then stored in a variable img (variables will be explained shortly). Then we create a sphere shape and set the texture image on the shape with the setTexture function. In Processing, every function "belongs" to something, and in the previous examples, all functions (like fill or ellipse) belong to the canvas itself. Since the canvas is the default drawing environment in Processing, we don't need to mention this. Now, in this example with globe.setTexture(img), we use a function that "belongs" to the shape globe. When we use it, this function will only apply to the shape. The dot expresses this relation between the shape globe and its function setTexture. We will see more of this later on in the book.

Reminder   The image needs to be imported into the same folder where the processing file is. Try to replace this "earth.jpg" image by another picture you have on your computer.

Draw textured globes in Processing's 3D environment

```
// set canvas size and ask for 3D canvas
size(640, 640, P3D);

// white background, no outline for shapes
background(255);
noStroke();

// load the texture image of the earth, and note
// this only works if you have an image 'earth.jpg'
// in the same folder as your Processing sketch
// (any image will do, though)
PImage img = loadImage("earth.jpg");

// create a shape and set the image as texture
PShape globe = createShape(SPHERE, 100);
globe.setTexture(img);
```

```
// from the left to right, draw the first 3D ellipse
translate(width/5, height/5, -50);
shape(globe);
// from the left to right, draw the second 3D ellipse
translate(width/5, height/5, 0);
shape(globe);
// from the left to right, draw the third 3D ellipse
translate(width/5, height/5, 50);
shape(globe);
```

In the preceding example, we draw three different spheres with the same image as the texture. If we use a texture for a 3D object, this means that the image is wrapped around the surface of the object. In this case, one image is loaded in Processing, and it is used as a texture for different 3D shapes. The exact image is left to you to choose. We used an image of a world map, so the three spheres look like miniature globes.

In the beginning of this chapter, we have just touched the many functions of Processing – both in 2D and 3D. We have seen how we can start experimenting with very simple forms and shapes and how we can play with visual elements to express our ideas. In the next part, we look into the canvas itself which will help us understand the drawing process. Also, this makes working with complex animations later on much easier.

2.2 Canvas secrets

The Processing canvas is not just the surface on which we draw. The digital canvas offers its own features for coding art. It also influences how we draw: we can scale, translate, and rotate the canvas before or during drawing and thereby influence how the next visual elements are drawn. Let's start with scaling.

2.2.1 Scaling visual elements

In art, scale can be explored to an extreme degree, for instance, Chuck Close's painting "Mark" is "realism in an unreal scale" [13]. And the use of proportion in art can be experimented with and developed as "the art of photomontage," like in Hannah Hoch's 1925 painting "Equilibre (Balance)." The proportion within the human body presents a "purposeful alteration of human proportion to make a political statement" [13].

In Processing, a visual element's scale is always relative to the canvas and its coordinate system. Scale values are specified as decimal percentages. For example, the function called scale(2.0) doubles the size of a shape, an increase to 200%, and scale(0.8) reduces the size to 80%. Another interesting possibility of the scale function is that it can take two (or even three) parameters.

Using the scale function

```
// scale horizontally and vertically by 130%
scale(1.3);

// scale horizontally by 130% and keep vertical scale
scale(1.3, 1);
```

This way, we can "stretch" or "squeeze" shapes just using the canvas scale function. There is, however, one thing we need to remember: the scale function does not actually scale the shapes. Instead, it scales the canvas for the following drawing operations. That means, using scale will leave the canvas scaled until the scaling is changed again. If we use scale multiple times, the results "add up": scaling first by 2.0 and then by 3.0 is the same as scaling once by 6.0. That means, scaling values multiply.

The following example shows the combination effect when several scale functions are used together in one piece of code:

Using `scale` several times in one piece of code

```
// set canvas size and background color
size(1200, 200);
background(208, 170, 208);

// draw circle and rectangle in original scale
stroke(246, 173, 113);
strokeWeight(5);
fill(113, 70, 132);
ellipse(705, 145, 355, 355);
rect(530, 20, 355, 235, 130);

// draw first scaled rectangle
scale(1.3, 1.4);
fill(113, 70, 132, 150);
rect(530, 20, 355, 175, 230);

// draw second scaled rectangle
scale(0.6);
fill(113, 70, 132, 60);
stroke(246, 173, 113, 80);
rect(530, 20, 355, 175, 230);
```

Tips   Not just the combined effect matters; changing the order of scale functions in the code will produce different results.

Before moving on to other canvas tricks, let's see what we can do to bring the canvas back to its original scaling (before the first application `scale`).

2.2.2 Resetting or restoring the canvas

Why would we want to restore the canvas to its original setting? Imagine that you draw 10 or 20 overlapping objects, each with its own scaling. Now, you realize that you need a different order of objects and you move them around. Suddenly, all the scaling is off because the effects of the different scaling operations influence each other (they "add up"; see earlier). What to do? We suggest scaling objects individually and always resetting the canvas before scaling and drawing the next object. This way, you can easily move around parts of your code without annoying side effects.

There are basically two ways in which we can reset the canvas to its original scaling (and translation and rotation). The first one is a straightforward call to `resetMatrix` as shown in the following example:

Reset any transformation to the original canvas

```
// scale canvas once and draw rectangle
scale(0.8);
rect(0, 0, 20, 20);

// reset canvas
resetMatrix();

// next scale, draw rectangle
scale(0.6);
rect(0, 0, 20, 20);
```

Tips   Of course, we can also restore the canvas by reversing previous scaling operations: `scale(0.8)` ... `scale(1.25)` (create restore point). However, this becomes cumbersome quickly.

This can be also described as a full reset, because it brings all settings back to the basic canvas settings, often called "defaults." Sometimes, we would like to separately control which canvas settings are rolled back and which remain. For this purpose, we can use the two functions `pushMatrix` and `popMatrix`. They should always come as a pair, with `pushMatrix` as the first. Push and pop work by first creating a restore point (push) and then restoring the canvas to exactly this point (pop). We can "stack up" multiple restore points, which are then restored in the opposite order in which they were "pushed" upon the stack. As an example, the restore points `point1`, `point2`, and `point3` are restored in the order: `point3`, `point2`, and finally `point1`.

With these two functions, we can selectively roll back canvas scaling, like in the following example:

Selectively roll back transformations with `pushMatrix` and `popMatrix`

```
// scale canvas once and draw rectangle
scale(0.8);
rect(0, 0, 20, 20);

// save canvas
pushMatrix();
// vertical stretch
scale(0.6, 1.2);
ellipse(10, 10, 20, 20);
// restore canvas from restore point
popMatrix();
```

35

```
// draw rectangle in same scaling as above
rect(30, 0, 20, 20);

// save canvas
pushMatrix();
// horizontal stretch
scale(1.2, 0.6);
ellipse(40, 10, 20, 20);
// restore canvas
popMatrix();
```

Reminder   If you write `pushMatrix`, directly write `popMatrix`, so you don't forget it later on. For advanced use cases, it is possible to nest `pushMatrix` and `popMatrix`. Always remember that both functions need to be called exactly in the right order ("first push, then pop") and also in the exactly same number of times.

2.2.3 Rotation and translation

There are two more canvas operations next to `scale` that we would like to introduce. `rotate` and `translate` are the functions used for spinning and moving visual elements. Actually, what happens is that the canvas is first moved or rotated and then the element is drawn. As a result, we see the moved or rotated element. All following elements will be drawn with the same canvas movement or rotation, unless we reset the canvas with `resetMatrix` or we use `pushMatrix` and `popMatrix` as shown before.

Let's illustrate this quickly with an example. We draw a black rectangle on a white canvas, at first without any transformation (scale, translate or rotate).

Step 1: Draw a black rectangle on a canvas without transformation

```
// setup canvas
size(200, 200);
background(0);
rectMode(CENTER);

// draw the white canvas
fill(255);
rect(width/2, height/2, 200, 200);

// draw black rectangle on canvas
fill(0);
rect(width/2, height/2, 40, 40);
```

Now, we rotate the white canvas and draw the black rectangle as before:

Step 2: Draw a black rectangle on a rotated white canvas

```
// setup canvas
size(200, 200);
background(0);
rectMode(CENTER);

// rotate canvas by 10 degrees
rotate(radians(10));

// draw the white canvas
fill(255);
rect(width/2, height/2, 200, 200);

// draw black rectangle on canvas
fill(0);
rect(width/2, height/2, 40, 40);
```

We see that both the white canvas and the black rectangle are rotated around the top-left corner. Any rotation in Processing will be relative to the origin of the canvas, which is by default the top-left corner at point (0, 0). If we want to rotate around a different point, we need to first translate the canvas to this point. This means we set the (0, 0) point of the canvas to this new location and then rotate. The next example shows how this works by leaving the white canvas out of the rotation and just rotating the black rectangle around its center point (which is also the center of the canvas at location (width/2, height/2)).

Step 3: Black rectangle on rotated and translated white canvas

```
// setup canvas
size(200, 200);
background(0);
rectMode(CENTER);

// draw the white canvas
fill(255);
rect(width/2, height/2, 200, 200);

// translate to center point
translate(width/2, height/2);

// rotate by 10 degrees
rotate(radians(10));

// draw black rectangle using the new (0, 0)
fill(0);
rect(0, 0, 40, 40);
```

We can combine different transformations as well, for instance, we can insert a scale just after translate to increase the size of the black rectangle.

Combining different transformations

```
// translate to center point
translate(width/2, height/2);
// scale the black rectangle by 150%
scale(1.5);
// rotate by 10 degrees
rotate(radians(10));
```

In the next example, we translate the same original circle to four different positions and scale down the canvas every time, so we see four shifted and smaller circles. The circles are drawn in transparent fill and stroke colors, so the effect is clearer.

Combining translate and scale repeatedly

```
// setup canvas
size(400, 400);
background(208, 170, 208);
fill(113, 70, 132, 100);
stroke(246, 173, 113, 100);
strokeWeight(5);

// draw the first ellipse
ellipse(150, 150, 150, 150);

// second ellipse shifted to right and scaled down
translate(50, 50);
scale(0.9);
ellipse(150, 150, 150, 150);
```

```
// third ellipse shifted and scaled again
translate(50, 50);
scale(0.9);
ellipse(150, 150, 150, 150);

// fourth ellipse shifted and scaled again
translate(50, 50);
scale(0.9);
ellipse(150, 150, 150, 150);
```

Reminder   Be careful with the order of your transformations.
`rotate` before `translate` has a different effect than the other
way around. You can reset the effects of canvas transformations
with `resetMatrix` or work more fine-grained with `pushMatrix` and
`popMatrix`. That's it.

What you need to remember from this section is that there are three
main transformations in Processing: `scale`, `translate`, and `rotate`. They
can be used together in any order, and you can stack them up, which means
that their effects sum up. Be careful: if you apply multiple transformations,
the ordering will have an effect. For example, if you first `translate`, then
`rotate` will look different from first `rotate` and then `translate`. Why?
Because the rotation point is translated in the first case, the second case
uses the original rotation point and translates after rotating.

Once we come to drawing with Processing in 3D space, you will see that
the transformations also work in 3D – just with more parameters. You can
shift, rotate, and scale any visual element in all three axes of the 3D space.

2.3 Animation: From frames to motion

What does "animation" mean when coding your idea? In this book, it is nothing more than painting frames so quickly in a sequence that the human mind perceives movement although it is literally stop motion. Almost all following examples use this technique. One of the first examples of using this technique was by the Lumière brothers already in 1895.

2.3.1 Animation basics

Before we can dive into animation, we need to introduce a mechanism that allows us to paint frames quickly. This is a necessary ingredient for animation. Processing is perfectly suited for this, as it even suggests the following structure for any Processing sketch. Let's see one example.

The general structure of programs in Processing

```
// the setup function is run only once
// set up canvas and drawing style here
void setup() {
  size(640, 640);

  background(208, 170, 208);
  stroke(246, 173, 113);
  fill(64, 72, 224);
}

// the draw function is run 30 or even 60 times per second
// and it draws a single frame
void draw() {
  // frame contents
  // ...
}
```

Tips   When you type the opening bracket '{', immediately type the closing one as well '}', so you don't forget it later on. Same for '(' and ')'.

The preceding code is the basic Processing structure that we will use in all code examples in the remainder of this book. We need to write two functions, setup and draw as a skeleton. What are functions? They are blocks of code that have a name and sometimes input values called "parameters". These blocks of code can be used once or many times. In Processing, functions surround code with curly brackets. We will explain functions in more detail later on in the book. For now, you can follow the example structure.

Processing can animate already with the two functions, setup and draw. This simple structure is enough to work with frame-by-frame animation. How does that work? When the Processing program starts, the setup function will be run once. This means that Processing will run the code between the curly brackets of the setup function. Here, you can place code to "set up" the scene and all important setting for the canvas when the program starts. The second function, draw, is what makes the frame-by-frame animation happen: the code inside the draw function is called many times per second and runs until the program stops. Usually, the draw function starts by erasing the background; otherwise, we would just draw over the previous frame.

What else is needed to actually see motion? A moving object or scene! The next section shows how we can easily animate a visual element.

2.3.2 Simple movement

As a first example of movement in animation, we move a small rectangle pixel by pixel to the right side of the canvas until it disappears.

Move a small rectangle pixel by pixel

```
void setup() {
  size(400, 400);
}

void draw() {
  // erase the background (= clean canvas)
  background(160);
  // draw rectangle at x-position given by frameCount
  rect(frameCount, 30, 10, 10);
}
```

Now we have a code structure with setup and draw, which divides the code into one piece that is run only once during the setup and another piece (the code in draw) that is run repeatedly. What is the other difference? We are using frameCount, a variable from Processing that simply counts how many frames have been drawn by draw since the start of the program. In the first run of draw, frameCount is 1, then 2, then 3, and so forth. When we use this variable to position the rectangle (as the value for the x coordinate), we move the rectangle every frame 1 pixel to the right. Because we do this fast enough, our perception is tricked, and we see a smoothly moving rectangle.

This is the secret of animation, in short, drawing frame by frame really fast and changing a little bit between the frames to construct an illusion of movement. For decades, traditional animations, from Walt Disney's first works to Studio Ghibli's breathtaking movies, were drawn frame by frame on papers by hundreds of talented visual artists. Now we can let Processing do this job on its digital canvas for us. Let's rotate the rectangle while we move it.

Move and rotate a small rectangle

```
void setup() {
  size(400, 400);
  rectMode(CENTER);
}

void draw() {
  background(160);
  // move rectangle by frameCount
  translate(frameCount, 30);
  // rotate rectangle
  rotate(radians(frameCount * (360 / (2 * PI * 10))));
  rect(0, 0, 20, 20);
}
```

In this second example, we combine the linear movement of the rectangle with two canvas operations: translate and rotate. Again, we use frameCount as the element of change between the frames, but now we use it twice: once for shifting and once for rotation. Let's first assume that we treat the rolling rectangle as a rolling circle. This makes the following calculations easier: we multiply frameCount with 360/(2∗π∗10) to achieve a rolling motion. This small formula relates the full rotation of 360° to the circle's circumference (calculated by 2∗π∗*radius*). The radius of the circle (10) is half of the circle's width. In other words, we relate the number of degrees (360) to the distance the circle has to travel during a full rotation (2∗π∗10).

This calculation is only one way to arrive at a motion that feels right. While it is nice to be able to calculate it, you could get there also by trusting your eyes and tweaking the values until it feels right. This is a good example of how we can achieve similar results in different ways. You should choose the one that you are most comfortable with – Processing never minds playing nice stuff for you.

2.3.3 Rhythm in motion

Motion can take different forms. It can be linear, it can be periodic, random, or entirely different and more complex. The preceding examples show linear motion along a horizontal line that leads the rectangle eventually out of the canvas. What if we would want the rectangle to stay with us? This section shows two examples that keep the visual element within the boundaries of the canvas.

The first one is a simple variation of the previous moving rectangle.

Add a variation when moving and rotating a small rectangle

```
void setup() {
  size(400, 400);
  rectMode(CENTER);
}

void draw() {
  background(160);
  translate(width/2, height/2);
  rotate(radians(frameCount * (360 / (2 * PI * 10))));
  rect(50, 0, 20, 20);
}
```

The only change is in translating into the center of the canvas and drawing the rectangle at a fixed distance of 50 pixels from the rotation point. The rectangle stays within the canvas simply because its path is now a circle and not a straight line anymore. Too simple? Agreed!

The next example is about using the increasing frameCount to create periodic motion. An easy way to do that is to wrap the frameCount with the sin function. The sin function is really helpful if we need a bit of a wiggling motion anywhere in Processing. If we feed it an increasing value like the frameCount, the sin function will turn it into a value that (smoothly) moves between -1 and 1.

Using the sin function

```
// use the increasing frame counter variable divided by 20
// to 'drive' the sin function
sin(frameCount/20.0)
```

? Think about this

Why do we use frameCount/20.0 instead of frameCount? Try to change the value frameCount/20.0, or the height 20 and the width 20 of this rectangle. What happens now?

Due to the nature of the sin function, the direct values of frameCount such as 0, 1, 2, 3, ... cause the output of the calculation to be a bit jumpy. Therefore, we divide the frameCount by 20.0. This way, the input to sin changes in smaller steps and output value becomes smoother – exactly what we need for the bouncing rectangle example. Still, it would not really work because the output of sin is in the range of -1 to 1, which would only be a tiny wiggle on the canvas. We can make this wiggling motion more visible by multiplying it with half the width of the canvas and translating the whole canvas by the same amount to the right. The full example shows how it works together.

Horizontal movement with the `sin` function

```
// setup as before
void draw() {
  background(160);
  translate(width/2, height/2);
  rect(sin(frameCount/20.0) * width/2, 20, 20, 20);
}
```

We combine linear and periodic motion in the following example. The lower rectangle simply follows the `frameCount` directly. The upper rectangle performs a bouncing motion which results from using the output of `sin` as before, but applying the abs function to it. The abs function simply leaves any positive value unchanged (1 stays 1) and turns any negative value into its positive counterpart (-1 becomes 1). When we apply this to the `sin` function, it starts bouncing instead of moving in a smooth wave.

Combining `abs` and `sin` function

```
// setup as before

void draw() {
  background(160);
  translate(0, height/2);

  // linear rectangle (lower position)
  rect(frameCount, 20, 20, 20);

  // bouncing rectangle (upper position)
  rect(frameCount, -1 * abs(sin(frameCount/20.0)) * 60, 20, 20);
}
```

Tips   For the dynamic rectangle, try to change the value `20.0` and `60` within `abs(sin(frameCount/20.0))*60` to see how to apply different types of motion to a same object.

You might have noticed a small final detail: we need to multiply the `abs` function with -1 because the vertical position in Processing canvas goes from 0 (top) to `height` (bottom). That is, the larger the vertical position, the closer it is to the bottom of the canvas. Effectively, multiplying with -1 turns the output of `abs` upside down, which fits the motion better. Try removing it and you will see the difference.

As a final example of periodic motion (Figure 2-4), we can create a snap-back motion for the lower rectangle of the previous example. Also, we change the `fill` color of both rectangles: when they seem to clash, they are darkest and then gradually becoming lighter.

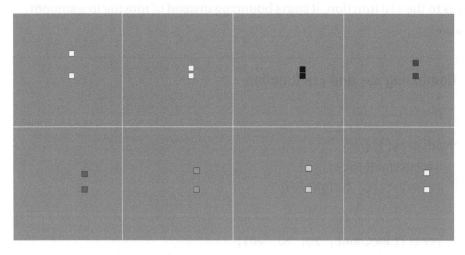

Figure 2-4. *Two color-changing rectangles in motion*

Adding a snap-back motion to the previous example

```
// setup as before

void draw() {
  background(160);
  translate(0, height/2);

  // change color according to frameCount
  fill(frameCount % (20 * PI) * 10);

  // bouncing rectangle (same as before)
  rect(frameCount, -1 * abs(sin(frameCount/20.0)) * 60, 20, 20);

  // linear rectangle with snap-back motion
  rect(frameCount, 20, 20, 20);
  translate(25, 15);
  rotate(radians(90 - (frameCount % (20 * PI))));
}
```

Again, we use simple formulas to calculate the relationship between the different parts of the animation: the synchronized snap-back movement of the lower rectangle and the synchronized color fading of both rectangles (Figure 2-5). For both of them, it is important to understand how the modulo operator % works: the modulo operator, in many programming languages denoted as %, returns the division rest. For example, if we divide 5 by 4, the division rest is 1; if we divide 4 by 4, it is 0. The following listing shows how it works:

The modulo operator

```
// example of modulo operator %
0 % 4 = 0          4 % 4 = 0          8 % 4 = 0
1 % 4 = 1          5 % 4 = 1          9 % 4 = 1
2 % 4 = 2          6 % 4 = 2          ...
3 % 4 = 3          7 % 4 = 3
```

With rising numbers before the % operator, the output is a rising sequence from 0 up to the value just before the operand (here 4). If you would describe this visually, you would see a sawtooth-like curve, which can be useful as another periodic form to control visual elements in Processing. We use it all the time.

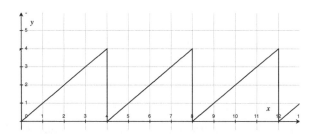

Figure 2-5. *The* modulo *operator visualized. Notice the distinctive "sawtooth" pattern*

2.4 Interaction as input for animation

What we have created so far are static or dynamic visual elements without reactions to input. That means, the Processing sketches will run by themselves. And While they run, we cannot control the visual outcome. In this short section, we will introduce how to use the mouse to control our visual elements. The first thing we need to understand is that any number that we have typed in Processing sketches so far can be controlled by input from an interaction like a mouse movement or mouse click. Check out the following example:

Using the mouse to control a visual element

```
void setup() {
  size(400, 400);
  rectMode(CENTER);
}

void draw() {
  background(160);

  // the first circle is static
  ellipse(50, 75, 50, 50);

  // the second circle is dynamic
  ellipse(mouseX, mouseY, 50, 50);
}
```

In this piece of code, we draw two ellipses on the canvas. The first ellipse is static; it will not move. For the second ellipse, we have replaced the first numbers 50 and 75 by mouseX and mouseY. When you try this in Processing, you will see that the second ellipse is now locked to the mouse pointer. In other words, the ellipse is drawn at the same position as the mouse pointer. The simple replacement of the static numbers by mouseX and mouseY changes the behavior of the ellipse: it will be positioned wherever mouseX and mouseY direct it.

How does this work? mouseX and mouseY are called variables. We have seen variables before. They are pieces of data that can change. How do they change in this case? Processing will automatically fill in the current mouse position, so we can use the current horizontal mouse position as mouseX and the vertical mouse position as mouseY.

? Think about this

Can you use the mouse position to control something else, for
instance, the rectangle size or the `fill` color? Try it and remember
this is just about replacing static numbers with a variable like
mouseX.

After this quick tryout, we will look into three interaction basics one
by one, linking with coding visual elements we mentioned earlier, to
explain the features of bringing together interaction and visual elements.

2.4.1 Combining mouse presses and movement

In Processing, mousePressed is another helpful variable that has only two
possible values: true and false. Processing will fill this in automatically
as soon as there is a new mouse press event registered by the mouse. In
the next example, the interaction is simply to press the left mouse button
down, hold it, and move the mouse to the desired position of the canvas
(often called "dragging the mouse").

Using the mousePressed function

```
void setup() {
  size(600, 600);
}
void draw() {
  // white background, black line color
  background(255);
  stroke(0);
```

```
// if the mouse is pressed, then ...
if (mousePressed) {
  // ... draw an interesting line
  line(mouseX, 150, 150, mouseY);
}
}
```

Tips   In Processing, any key press can play the same role as a mouse button. Try to replace `mousePressed` with `keyPressed` in this piece of code. Can you figure out from the Processing reference how to distinguish different keys?

In this example, we combine the pressing of the left mouse button and mouse movement to draw a simple line. What is also new in this example is the use of an `if` statement that checks a condition before drawing the line on the canvas. These `if` statements evaluate a condition that is given in the parentheses. In this case, it evaluates whether `mousePressed` is `true`. If so, the line is actually drawn; otherwise, nothing happens.

We will see later how to use `mousePressed` in different ways, for instance, to switch elements or activate different parts of a Processing sketch.

2.5 Summary

This chapter was about experimenting with Processing to find visual elements that we like and find interesting. We have seen that we can easily work with one or two visual elements. However, working with many of them can easily become complex. If we want to change one feature of all shapes, we would need to edit many lines of code. There should be a way to solve this kind of problem without typing too much and letting the machine do most of the work.

In the next step – COMPOSITION AND STRUCTURE – we will explain how to do this with structure and style, so you can develop your Processing sketch into a more complex artwork. Yes, we will learn about unleashing the machine's power without losing control as a creator.

CHAPTER 3

Composition and structure

In the previous chapter, we started with drawing visual elements with and experimented with these elements in Processing, line by line. In this chapter, we move from the first step toward the second step: COMPOSITION AND STRUCTURE. The longer we experiment with visual elements and the more we discover about their properties, the more complex become the sketches we can create. For example, we can create variants of an interesting visual element when quickly trying out different shapes, color combinations, and form compositions. In the beginning, this creative progress is fast, but then it slows down because our sketches get more and more complex. We can experience this as feeling "stuck," overwhelmed or confused. One way to move on is to add some kind of order or structure, so our minds can relax and build up momentum for the next steps. Structure is not just helpful to regain an overview and make sense of code. Structure is also an aesthetic quality and can help us express our ideas by focusing on the bigger picture or the relations between visual elements or visual layers.

In this chapter, we show you how to work with visual structure using repetition, variation, and randomness and also how to let your ideas grow toward a first prototype. Before going into the details of visual structure, we will take a look how you can structure code and data and how you can

© Yu Zhang, Mathias Funk 2021
Y. Zhang and M. Funk, *Coding Art*, https://doi.org/10.1007/978-1-4842-6264-1_3

extend visual control from individual visual elements to many elements or things. By deconstructing "many things," we may have a preparation of going into the visual structures in the later sections.

3.1 Data and code structure

When extending the first sketches of an idea, we can start by increasing the number of existing visual elements, add variations, and play with a multitude of elements before reducing to the final set of absolutely necessary elements. The creative act of expanding the collection of visual elements often generates new ideas and perspectives.

This section is divided into two parts: "creating many things" and "controlling many things." We will start by extending the range of visual elements to "many things." This is about creating many variations or clones of a single visual element and how these clones can be displayed and controlled.

Every programming language contains one or more features to work with many objects at the same time. This is something that computers do really well: apply the same or similar instructions to multiple objects as fast as possible. So, for the creative, it is merely the challenge to tell the computer exactly what needs to be done. It's best to see it live: here and now, we will make particles and animate them.

3.1.1 Creating many things

A first example of how to create many things on a Processing canvas is the random generation of dots on the defined canvas:

Randomly generate dots

```
void setup() {
  size(400, 400);
```

```
  background(35, 27, 107);
  noStroke();
}

void draw() {
  fill(238, 120, 138, 250);
  ellipse(random(0, width), random(0, height), 15, 15);

  filter(BLUR, 1);
}
```

We would like to draw the exactly same shape, but with slightly different features. In the next example, we create two variables x and y for the position. In a way, we first set the position variables before we draw the ellipse at that position in the draw function.

Randomly generate dots with two variables x and y

```
void draw() {
  fill(238, 120, 138, 250);
  // create two variables x, y for position
  float x = random(0, width);
  float y = random(0, height);
  ellipse(x, y, 15, 15);
  filter(BLUR, 1);
}
```

Let's do a further small exercise based on this example. In the previous examples, the dots cover the entire canvas. What if we want to draw the dots only inside a circle in the center of the canvas? We can do this by adding only a little more code (Figure 3-1).

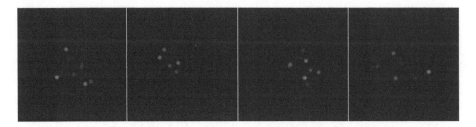

Figure 3-1. *Draw fading dots in the center of the canvas*

How to specify positions for many things drawn on the canvas

```
void draw() {
  fill(238, 120, 138, 250);
  // create two variables x, y for position
  float x = random(0, width);
  float y = random(0, height);
  // check that distance between (x,y) and canvas
  // center is less than 150, only then draw ellipse
  if (dist(x, y, width/2, height/2) < 150) {
    ellipse(x, y, 15, 15);
  }
  filter(BLUR, 1);
}
```

This example introduced the dist function that basically returns the pixel distance between two points. These two points are given by their x and y coordinates (in the order: first point x and y, then second point x and y). The if condition ensures that we only draw a dot if the dot's distance to the center point is less than 150 pixels (in this example). Not too difficult, right? This technique is sometimes called "generate and test," because we generate positions randomly and then test if they match our distance criterion. Only with a match the positions are actually used and a shape is painted.

What happens in these sketches in terms of "many things"? After the simple setup of the canvas, we draw one ellipse per frame at a random location. The filter at the end blurs the canvas, so that the ellipses become more and more blurred until they disappear. We do not erase the background in this sketch, which results in layered drawing and blurring. While we are drawing what appears to be "many things" here, we are basically drawing a single ellipse and only the canvas visually "remembers" it. We lose touch with the individual ellipse after it has been drawn.

To be more in control, we need to find a way to remember the ellipse (or its position) in the code structure and to change it. At the same time, we need to remember and draw multiple ellipses, so we can create new visuals composed of multiple ellipses.

In the next example, we will store 60 ellipses by means of their position and draw them in a loop. When we click the mouse, the mouse position will be stored as the position for the currently selected ellipse. This way, we can draw looping figures on the canvas and try it out first; the details will be explained shortly.

Draw an interactive mouse trace

```
PVector[] ellipses = new PVector[60];

void setup() {
  size(400, 400); background(35, 27, 107); noStroke();

  // initialize the array ellipses
  for (int i = 0; i < ellipses.length; i++) {
    ellipses[i] = new PVector();
  }
}

void draw() {
  filter(BLUR, 1);
```

```
// pick one position from the array
PVector p = ellipses[frameCount % ellipses.length];

// set mouse position if mouse is pressed
if (mousePressed) {
  p.set(mouseX, mouseY);
}

// draw the position
fill(238, 120, 138, 250);
ellipse(p.x, p.y, 15, 15);
}
```

? Think about this

You remember from before that a PVector object packages the x and y coordinates of a position, right? You can read and also write the coordinate individually and also use more advanced operations. We will come back to this soon.

How does this "storing" work? In Processing and many other programming languages, we use an array for storing multiple objects of the same type, such as the position that is given here as a PVector object. Arrays are defined by using square brackets and a number for the size. In the case of the ellipses array, we use 60 for the size (see the first line of the preceding code).

Tips   There are also other types of loops, but we are using only the for loop in this book. The Processing reference has more information if you are interested.

Now we have memory space for 60 positions. The next thing we need to do is initialize the space with actual positions, that is, instances of PVector. This happens in the setup method inside a loop. Loops are a new concept that make a lot of sense when using arrays. Ok, so what are loops? Loops allow us to execute the same code (inside the loop) for a specific number of times, and we need exactly that for initializing the array: creating a PVector object 60 times. This loop is a for loop that uses a counter i and a condition (execute loop as long as i is smaller than 60). The loop starts with i = 0, and, every time it runs, it increases by 1 with i++.

Finally, we can use the 60 different positions in the draw method where we pick one position to draw an ellipse at this position. Before we draw the ellipse, we check whether the mouse is currently pressed (mousePressed). If that is the case, we update the position in the array with the current mouse position. With this change, we can now draw on the canvas, and the positions remember our drawing and repeat it until we press the mouse again and set a new position.

Let's try another example of creating many things. This time, we go for "thousands of things" (see Figure 3-2). In this example, we create 4000 particles. Each particle has a position and size (see the particle variable) and a direction of movement (see the direction). We use the Processing PVector data type as way to store the position and size in one PVector object and the direction in another PVector object.

Draw 4000 particles in motion

```
// reserve memory space for 4000 particle positions
PVector[] particle = new PVector[4000];
// reserve memory space for 4000 particle directions
PVector[] direction = new PVector[4000];
void setup() {
```

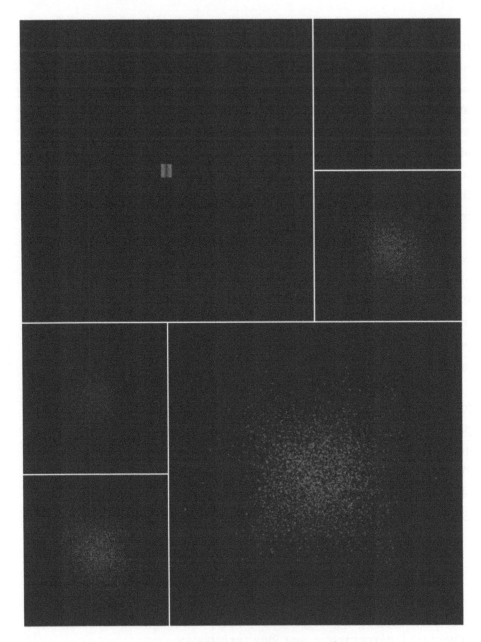

Figure 3-2. *Draw 4000 particles in a direction of movement*

```
  size(600, 600); smooth(); noStroke();
  // loop through all 4000 particles
  for (int i = 0; i < 4000; i++) {
    // initialize particle at center position with a third
    // component for size and color of the particle
    particle[i] = new PVector(0, 0, random(0.5, 4));
    // initialize random particle direction
    direction[i] = new PVector(random(-1, 1), random(-1, 1));
  }
}

void draw() {
  // dark blue background
  background(35, 27, 107);
  // always draw from center of canvas
  translate(width/2, height/2);

  // loop through all particles
  for (int i = 0; i < 4000; i++) {
    // change position
    PVector p = particle[i].add(direction[i]);
    // adjust individual color
    fill(238, 120, 138, p.z * 30);
    // draw particle shape
    ellipse(p.x, p.y, p.z, p.z);
  }
}
```

In this example, we use a trick to store all the different properties of a particle in two different arrays. This can get confusing, because we always need to initialize, read, and update both arrays. So, here is a better way: Processing allows us to define our own data structure for a particle. In the following code, you can see how we changed the previous sketch.

Use a data structure to define particles

```
// reserve memory space for 4000 particles
Particle[] particles = new Particle [4000];
void setup() {
  size(600, 600); smooth(); noStroke();
  // loop through all 4000 particles and initialize
  for (int i = 0; i < 4000; i++) {
    particles[i] = new Particle();
  }
}
void draw() {
  // dark blue background
  background(35, 27, 107);
  // always draw from center of canvas
  translate(width/2, height/2);
  // loop through all particles
  for (Particle p : particles) {
    // change position and draw particle
    p.move();
    p.show();
  }
}
// create a new class for our particle
class Particle {
  float x, y, size, directionX, directionY;
  // initialize (called 'constructor')
  public Particle() {
    this.size = random(0.5, 4);
    this.directionX = random(-1, 1);
    this.directionY = random(-1, 1);
  }
```

```
// function to move the particle position in direction
public void move() {
  // add directionX to x, and directionY to y
  this.x += directionX;
  this.y += directionY;
}
// draw the particle on the Processing canvas
public void show() {
  // set individual particle color
  fill(238, 120, 138, this.size * 30);
  // draw particle shape
  ellipse(this.x, this.y, this.size, this.size);
}
}
```

In the first lines, we do not create two arrays anymore. Instead, we create a single array of Particle which is then initialized in the setup function. The new Particle class is shown at the bottom of the sketch. We define five variables (x, y, size, directionX, directionY) and three functions inside this class. The first function Particle() is called a constructor, and it will automatically be called when Processing creates an instance of this class. This is useful for setting up the variables inside. Two more functions, move and show, allow us to move and draw a single particle on the screen. A bit like a remote control.

After setting up the class, you can see in the draw function how we use it: we loop through all particles and call the move and show functions for every single particle. The draw function is now nicely short and simple. This is an example how we also use the structure to simplify our code: we separate the code into the control part in the draw loop and movement and drawing code inside the Particle class.

3.1.2 Controlling many things

The previous example shows how to create many things and a first view on how to control them. Thanks to the simplified structure with the Particle class, we can now change just the move function to keep particles on the canvas and prevent them from moving out of the screen. The following code just replaces the move function in the previous example.

Change the move function to control many things

```
public void move() {
    // calculate the particle's distance from the center
    if (dist(this.x, this.y, 0, 0) > 250) {
        // create position and new random target position
        PVector position = new PVector(this.x, this.y);
        PVector target = new PVector(random(-250, 250), random
            (-250, 250));
        // calculate direction vector between
        // current and target position
        PVector direction = PVector.sub(target, position);
        // divide direction by 600 to make the steps small
        direction.div(600);
        // set the new direction for the particle
        directionX = direction.x;
        directionY = direction.y;
    }
    // this is as before
    this.x += directionX;
    this.y += directionY;
}
```

In this example, we limit the movement of particles with an invisible wall around the center of the canvas. How? Actually there is no "wall," but instead, we check how far away each particle is from the center point (0, 0). If the particle's distance to the center is 250 pixels or more, we immediately calculate a new direction for the particle to move to. So, every particle is now limited in their movement because it will automatically bounce back when it reaches the maximum distance to the center. And because all particles have the same limitation, we see an invisible wall. This is essentially the power of working with "many things."

This previous example shows how we can control the movement of many things by defining functions inside the new `Particle` class that allow to control one particle at a time. Since we have now a function to just control the movement of the particle, we can also use this to add interactivity.

? Think about this

Try changing the shape of the particles individually. For instance, whenever the particle bounces against the wall, it changes from dot to square and back.

Use mouse interactivity to control many things

```
// ...

void draw() {
  // dark blue background
  background(35, 27, 107);
  // always draw from center of canvas
  translate(width/2, height/2);
  // loop through all particles
```

```
  for (Particle p : particles) {
    // change position depending on the distance
    // of the mouse to the horizontal center
    p.move(abs(width/2 - mouseX));
    // draw particle
    p.show();
  }
}

// ...

// move function with additional parameter 'radius'
// that replaces the number 250 below
public void move(int radius) {
    // calculate the particle's distance from the center
    if (dist(this.x, this.y, 0, 0) > radius) {
      // create position and new random target position
      PVector position = new PVector(this.x, this.y);
      PVector target = new PVector(random(-radius, radius),
          random(-radius, radius));
      // calculate direction vector between
      // current and target position
      PVector direction = PVector.sub(target, position);
      // divide direction by 600 to make the steps small
      direction.div(600);
      // set the new direction for the particle
      directionX = direction.x;
      directionY = direction.y;
    }
```

```
    // this is as before
    this.x += directionX;
    this.y += directionY;
  }
  // ...
```

In this last example, we just change the previous code in two places: in the draw function, we call the move function with an additional parameter. This parameter is defined in the move function as radius and controls the maximal pixel distance from the center point. With this simple change, we can now control the invisible wall with the mouse. Try it out.

As a quick recap of the examples so far, we have worked with "many things" from creating to controlling them. We only use a single shape (a dot) to draw each particle, and the particle color and size are same for every particle. We can change this inside the show function of the Particle class. Finally, we control the overall shape of the particle cloud by using the mouse and its distance to the center.

Creating and controlling many things directly one by one needs some form of structure. Why? Imagine that you would have to create small variables and code snippets for 4000 particles. You would need to write a lot of code and keep thousands of things in mind to check and improve. If you would make a single mistake and copy it 4000 times, that would be a major problem to fix.

By using the array as a data structure and a for loop to access all the array elements, we can radically simplify the code need to control and draw all elements. At first, we use two different arrays with Processing's PVector data type as our data structure. Later, we introduce the class concept to combine information about a particle and to define functions to control its movement. The class Particle keeps different pieces of data of a particle together, so whatever we need for drawing a particle is all in one place. We can also modify the particle data. For example, we move the elements slightly before we draw it and create an animation of flying particles. The `class` structure also allows us to control the behavior of every particle with a simple function `move` and to draw it with `show`. Now we can achieve independent movement of all particles and still let them move according to general rules (think of the "invisible wall" here). The functions inside the `Particle` class have access to the memory of the particle. We can even add extra information for drawing such as the `radius`. This extra information is called parameter, and it allows to inject data into the behavior when we need it.

In a creative process, we can always start with less structure and then create more structure when things get complicated. If you often struggle with this, dedicate moments in your process to improve the structure, so you can be sure that you will be able to make good progress over time. Now that we used a better structure for data and code at the level of individual particles, what if we want to work with the entire cloud of particles directly? What if we want to create with structure in a more visual way?

3.2 Visual structure

Space is an indispensable component in visual art. Spatial positioning and layers give ways of controlling how visual elements appear and how their spatial interplay guides our perspective and attention. Visual structure in this chapter is about how we can compose elements or collections of elements visually, so they create relationships between each other. The topic of this section is to see the many things as one thing and to creatively work with it. Perhaps you have heard of Gestalt theory.[1] This is what we are using here: we create and manipulate a Gestalt.

---

[1]https://en.wikipedia.org/wiki/Gestaltpsychology

3.2.1 Composition and alignment

How to start with visual structure? Let's take the example from the previous section, the particle cloud, and compose it spatially. We will simply take the particle cloud and repeat it in six facets. In this example, we can combine concepts that we have seen before: translating the canvas and functions to reduce complexity. Many artists have worked with this kind of composition, essentially tiling the original image and thereby filling the entire canvas with repetitions that vary more or less from the original.

Replace the draw function in the previous example with the new version of the draw function and an additional function drawParticleCloud:

Draw particle clouds with a separate function `drawParticleCloud`

```
void draw() {
  // dark blue background
  background(35, 27, 107);
  // draw the particle cloud in different locations
  // (coordinates give the center points of the clouds)
  // first row (y coordinate --> 100)
  drawParticleCloud(100, 100);
  drawParticleCloud(300, 100);
  drawParticleCloud(500, 100);
  // second row (y coordinate --> 300)
  drawParticleCloud(100, 300);
  drawParticleCloud(300, 300);
  drawParticleCloud(500, 300);
}
```

```
// function to draw the particle cloud
// with location parameters
void drawParticleCloud(int x, int y) {
  // save canvas before translate
  pushMatrix();
  // translate to center of particle cloud
  translate(x, y);
  // loop through all particles
  for (Particle p : particles) {
    // change position and draw particle
    p.move(abs(width/2-mouseX));
    p.show();
  }
  // restore canvas
  popMatrix();
}
```

? Think about this

How to change the speed of the particles? Hint: You need to look into the Particle class and the move function.

We draw the particle cloud six times in two rows of three clouds. The preceding code adds a function drawParticleCloud that draws the particle cloud in a specific location. If we look closely, the particles move faster now and the animation seems to be a bit choppy. There are two reasons for that: first, we are drawing six clouds at the same time. That's 24000 instead of 4000 particles. This takes the computer more time to draw every frame: although drawing a tiny particle is really fast, drawing six times as many will add up. Depending on the processing power of our computer, the frame rate will go down. Why? For a frame rate of 60 frames per second, your computer needs to draw a single frame in about 16 milliseconds. If drawing this high number of particles takes longer than 16 milliseconds, then the frame cannot be drawn 60 times per second. As a result, the frame rate will go down and we see a slightly stuttery animation. The second reason is that we move every particle six times per frame, because we call the drawParticleCloud function six times every frame. All in all, not so nice.

How can we fix these problems? We can draw the particle cloud once and copy it directly to the other five areas. This is a quick change to the previous code that speeds up the animation immediately. The following code replaces the draw function as before:

Copying the cloud drawn by the drawParticleCloud function

```
void draw() {
  // dark blue background
  background(35, 27, 107);

  // first row
  drawParticleCloud(100, 100);
  copy(0, 0, 200, 200, 200, 0, 200, 200);
  copy(0, 0, 200, 200, 400, 0, 200, 200);
  // second row
  copy(0, 0, 200, 200, 0, 200, 200, 200);
  copy(0, 0, 200, 200, 200, 200, 200, 200);
  copy(0, 0, 200, 200, 400, 200, 200, 200);
}
```

Now we see clearly that the particle drawing only happens once in the code, followed by five calls to the copy function. The copy function in Processing works on the canvas directly and copies a rectangular area of the canvas into another area of the same canvas. The first four parameters are always the same in our example and specify the area that should be copied: "from position (0, 0), copy an area that is 200 by 200 pixels big."

The remaining four parameters specify the location and size of where the copy should be placed: "at position (200, 0), draw the copy in an area of size 200 by 200."

We can also copy the cloud that we draw directly into an image. After that, we can draw this image five times on the canvas. The result is the same as before, but now we have the cloud as a separate image and can change it before drawing it. Let's see what we can do with a little bit of tint.

Copying an image, drawing with tint effect

```
void draw() {
  // dark blue background
  background(35, 27, 107);

  // first row
  drawParticleCloud(100, 100);
  // copy cloud as image
  PImage cloud = get(0, 0, 200, 200);
  tint(255, 255, 200);
  image(cloud, 200, 0, 200, 200);
  tint(255, 255, 160);
  image(cloud, 400, 0, 200, 200);
  // second row
  tint(200, 160, 160);
  image(cloud, 0, 200, 200, 200);
  tint(200, 120, 80);
  image(cloud, 200, 200, 200, 200);
  tint(200, 80, 40);
  image(cloud, 400, 200, 200, 200);
}
```

The preceding code replaces the draw function. Before each image call, we use tint, which takes color values as parameters and changes the color tone of the next drawn images. A neutral tint would be using RGB values of (255, 255, 255), and you can even use transparency (fourth parameter) to draw transparent images. In the preceding code, we use RGB values to change the color tone for each image of the cloud. In the first row, we change toward a darker shade of blue (gradually lower values of the B part), and in the second row, we also reduce the amount of green (gradually lower values for the G part) to bring out the red in the particles more.

Changing the color tone is one example of what you can do with the image of the particle cloud. You can use different filter functions, scale, or rotate the image before drawing it onto the canvas. It is important to understand that you apply these functions to the entire particle cloud which has been rendered as an image. All particles are projected onto a single layer (the image), and we can now manipulate this layer, but not individual particles anymore. By doing this, we speed up the rendering and gain interesting possibilities to manipulate the cloud as an image, but we lose the possibility to change individual particles. This is called an optimization: we optimize (make better) for speed and for being able to use functions like tint or filter. We can do this because we move our focus from individual particles to the whole cloud. In the next section, we will go one step further and explore how we can combine or compose multiple clouds.

3.2.2 Composing with layers

Over the centuries, painters have worked with layers to create perspective and depth. When painting a landscape, a still life, or even a portrait, one technique is to start from the edges of the canvas. Then you draw the background to the middle until the close range is in sight. You end with the details. Such a process is naturally based on layers. Layers help with the composition of objects in space, and they are used both in traditional painting and digital drawing tools. For example, using an application like Photoshop or Illustrator becomes a lot more powerful with layers: you can try out alternatives on separate layers, show or hide layers, and change their order. Essentially, by grouping visual elements into layers, we can let new relationships between visual elements emerge on the canvas.

In Processing, we distinguish the 2D and 3D drawing modes. We mentioned them earlier when talking about the positioning of elements and canvas operations. The 2D drawing mode is generally a collage; that means the first elements in the code will be drawn first and all following elements on top. In other words, when drawing layers on the 2D sketch surface, layers are drawn in the order of code statements in the draw function.

When drawing in Processing's 3D mode, this ordering in code is not important anymore. Instead, every element we draw is automatically positioned in 3D space (with x, y, z coordinates). How the elements are rendered depends on our viewing perspective, through the 3D camera. The computer will calculate which elements are visible from the camera perspective and then render just these elements. This means we can use the x, y, z axis, especially z depth of objects in 3D space with the P3D renderer without having to think about the order too much. Again, how to use the P3D renderer? Include it in the size call, like this: size(600, 600, P3D). See the next code example.

To better understand the concept of layers and how rich their composition can be, let's look at the particles again. In the following example (Figure 3-3), we reuse the code from the previous sections and replace the draw function. As before, we draw the particle cloud only once and then copy it into an image. We draw this image as a texture in a loop, which results in a long "tail" of slightly scaled copies that wiggles around slowly.

Composing layers in 3D

```
void setup() {
  // use the 3D renderer
  size(600, 600, P3D);
  // ...
}

void draw() {
  // dark blue background
  background(35, 27, 107);
  noStroke();
  // first row
  drawParticleCloud(100, 100);
  // get cloud as image
  PImage cloud = get(0, 0, 200, 200);
  // erase background again
  background(25, 17, 87);
  // move to center of canvas
  translate(width/2, height/2, 100 - frameCount/100.);
  // introduce slow rotation, so we can see everything
  rotateX(frameCount/300.);
  // draw 100 textured squares in a loop
  for (int i = 0; i < 100; i++) {
    // gradually scale down size
    scale(0.95, 0.95, 0.95);
    translate(0, 0, -100);
    // rotate on the x axis
    rotateY(radians(sin(frameCount/300.)) * 8);
    // draw square
    beginShape();
    // set cloud as texture
```

```
    texture(cloud);
    // almost invisible stroke
    stroke(255, 20);
    vertex(-100, -100, 0, 0, 0);
    vertex(100, -100, 0, 200, 0);
    vertex(100, 100, 0, 200, 200);
    vertex(-100, 100, 0, 0, 200);
    endShape(CLOSE);
  }
}
```

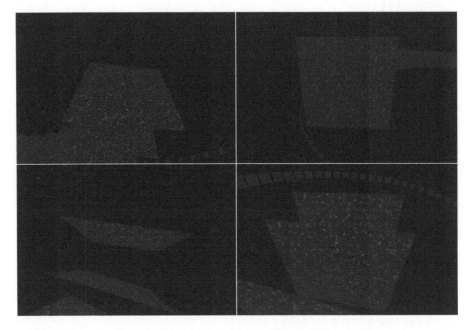

Figure 3-3. Composing layers in 3D that appear as a "tail"

The "tail" appears because every copy is shifted backward slightly in the z axis (note the translate(0, 0, -100) inside the for loop), and we scale down every time when we draw a copy, so the "tail" gets thinner and

thinner. Before drawing every copy, we also apply a slight rotation in the
y axis (note the rotateY(radians(sin(frameCount/300.))*8)), which
follows the sine function of the frameCount. This example shows how we
can simply layer elements such as the particle cloud image in space and
create visual elements from that (a "tail," for instance).

We have played with the particle cloud for some time now, but we have
never really looked inside. The particle cloud is made of layers as well. The
following example draws a single particle cloud in 3D space (again make
sure you use the P3D renderer with the size function). To use this code,
just replace the draw and show functions in the code from before.

Drawing a single particle cloud in 3D space

```
void draw() {
  // dark blue background, no stroke
  background(35, 27, 107);
  noStroke();
  // move canvas into position
  translate(width/2, height/2, -400);
  rotateY(radians(frameCount));
  // draw a single particle cloud
  for (Particle p : particles) {
    // change position and draw particle
    p.move(250);
    p.show();
  }
}
// change the following in class Particle
public void show() {
  // adjust individual color
  fill(238, 120, 138, this.size * 100);
  // save canvas
```

```
pushMatrix();
// translate
translate(0, 0, this.size * 200);
// draw particle shape
ellipse(this.x, this.y, this.size, this.size);
// draw transparent particle 'halo'
fill(238, 120, 138, this.size * 20);
ellipse(this.x, this.y, this.size * 20, this.size * 20);
// restore canvas
popMatrix();
}
```

In all the previous examples, we took a frontal view at the particle cloud. In the last example, we rotate it and see that can be far more interesting: a layered cake with differently colored particles from back to front. How did we do that? Each particle moves in its own layer, and we pull the layers a bit apart in the z axis (translate (0, 0, this.size * 200)). So, the specific size of a particle controls how far we move it in the z direction. Another change is that we draw each particle with a small transparent disc around it ("halo") that shows the layer orientation better than just a particle dot. We also disable the influence of the mouse position on the movement by calling move with a constant value of 250. We will bring back the mouse in the next section to control the visibility of different layers.

3.2.3 Controlling layers

In the previous two sections, we have created and composed layers. That means we have organized lots of particles in clouds and then worked with the clouds directly. We have seen how we can render and draw the clouds as images. Also, a particle cloud can be seen as consisting of multiple layers inside. What we have not really explored yet is how we can control the different layers.

In the following example (Figure 3-4), we will use the previous example and make it interactive. We control the visibility of all layers by the mouse position. To do this, we change only one small thing in the draw function: we wrap the existing p.show() in an if statement. This statement decides whether the layer depth (p.size) of the individual particle (scaled to the width of the window) is smaller than the horizontal position of the mouse (mouseX). Only if this is the case, the code inside the statement is executed. So, by moving the mouse, you can adjust how many layers of particles will be shown. Try it out!

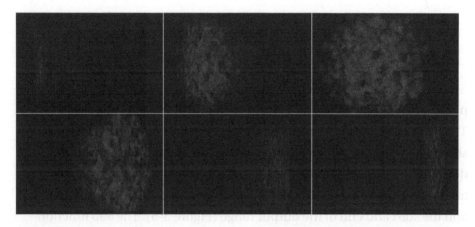

Figure 3-4. Control the visibility of the different layers with the mouse position

Control the visibility of layers with the mouse position

```
void draw() {
  // dark blue background, no stroke
  background(35, 27, 107);
  noStroke();
  // move canvas into position
  translate(width/2, height/2, -400);
  rotateY(radians(frameCount/1.));
```

```
// draw a single particle cloud
for (Particle p : particles) {
  // change position and draw particle
  p.move(250);
  // check if particle should be visible:
  // particle layer (scaled size property) is
  // smaller than horizontal mouse position
  if (map(p.size, 0.5, 2, 0, width) < mouseX) {
    p.show();
  }
 }
}
```

We can now move the mouse to show more or fewer layers of our particle cloud. We effectively control each layer's visibility at particle level. That means before drawing each particle, we check whether its layer should be visible or not given the current horizontal mouse position. How does this check work exactly? We use the map function, which takes five arguments: the value to be mapped, the start and end of the input range, and the start and end of the output range (Figure 3-5). The map function will then map the value from the input range to the output range. For example, it maps 4 from the input range [0..5] to 8 in the output range [0..10]. In our example, we map the size of a particle in range [0.5..2] to the entire width of the canvas [0..width] and then check whether this mapped value is smaller than the horizontal mouse position.

With a single additional line of code, we can bring back mouse control and turn this sketch into an interactive 3D experience. More importantly, we show how we can interactively control layers by tracking the mouse pointer and comparing its horizontal position to the mapped particle depth (p.size), which then determines whether the particle should be visible or not.

For the last part of this chapter, we zoom out from individual particles and their layers and look again at the whole cloud. In the last example, we show how to construct visual relationships between particles on different layers, while leaving the layers open for interaction.

The code for this example is again a replacement for the draw function and changes the following aspects: first, we change the type of for loop to go through the particles. The previous examples all used a for loop that directly iterates on the array elements. This example iterates with a counter i, which allows us to address the position of the current particle p and pair it with another particle q in the array. Particle q is chosen by subtracting particle p's index from the end of the array. So, if particle p is the first element, q is the last element. If p is the second element, q is the second last element, and so forth.

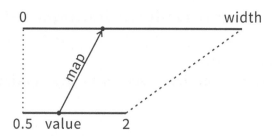

Figure 3-5. Explanation of the mapping between the input range and the output range. The input range (0.5-2) is given as follows and any value in this range is mapped to the corresponding value in the output range (0-width)

Constructing visual relationships between particles on layers

```
void draw() {
  // dark blue background, no stroke
  background(35, 27, 107); noStroke();
  // move canvas into position
```

```
translate(width/2, height/2, -400);
rotateY(radians(frameCount/1.));
// draw a single particle cloud
for (int i = 0; i < particles.length; i++) {
  Particle p = particles[i];
  // check the particle's z-property for threshold
  // set by mouse horizontal position
  if (mouseX <= map(p.size, 0.6, 2, 0, width)) {
    // change position and draw particles in the wider radius
    p.move(250);
    // draw without borders
    noStroke();
    p.show();
    // get paired particle q
    Particle q = particles[particles.length -1-i];
    // draw a transparent white line between p and q
    stroke(255, 30);
    line(p.x, p.y, p.size * 200, q.x, q.y, q.size * 200);
  } else {
    // set zero radius for particles that are not rendered
    p.move(0);
  }
}
}
```

We connect all paired particles with a semi-transparent white line – if at least one of the two particles in the pair is visible. The second change is that we set the movement radius for all invisible particles (below the mouse filter threshold) to 0, which causes them to slowly move to the center of the particle cloud. And because they are not visible, we see that the white lines converge into a sharp angle. The moment we display more or even all layers, the particles on the converged layers start to expand and the cloud opens up like an exotic flower. It's worth playing with for a while.

3.3 Summary

In this chapter, we went from drawing individual visual elements to drawing many of them. We use the computer's power to perform similar operations fast and to work efficiently with structured data. The important lesson here is: as soon as we can structure our creative input in such a way that the computer can understand it and execute it fast, we can use its power to draw things that would take us ages to do manually.

In creative practice, we intuitively shift, mix, blend, transform, and group layers. We can now create complex visual designs by coding element by element and layer by layer. We explored different visual dynamics within each layer. We compose layers to see how the overall composition will represent your idea. We need to do this in iterations of coding, running, reflecting, and coding again to deeply consider the dynamic connection between different visual layers and perception of these layers.

As a motivation for the next step, we can now move many things around and also let them behave in a very controlled way using calculated parameters. All nice, but it seems a bit "flat" in the sense that we can, after a short while already, understand and predict the motions of all particles. What if we had access to some randomness and noise that would create variations in the machine's work, so it would look less mechanical? Also, how to influence our creations live and in real time? Can we build our own brushes, colors, and canvases so we can intuitively create with the help of the machine as it knows how we want it to work? And how can we introduce interaction to our creative works? We can; just follow us to the next step.

CHAPTER 4

Refinement and depth

In this chapter, we will shape up visual elements and implement visual structure together with code structure. Visual elements can evolve best when the idea is still under construction, and we can follow new inspirations from working with code. We will also dig a bit deeper in working with data structures and unleash new powers of Processing. To achieve this, we introduce four refinements here: "Randomness and Noise," "MemoryDot," "Using Computed Values," and "Interaction." Using these refinements, we can make big steps from the simple visual elements of the previous step toward solutions that match our idea even better.

Let's start with some randomness, and you will soon get an idea of how to let the computer do more for you.

4.1 Randomness and noise

We have seen randomness before in this book. Every time we use random in our code, we use randomness. But what is that exactly? A number is random if it cannot be predicted from previous numbers. Also when we generate random numbers between 1 and 5, for example, each of these numbers 1, 2, 3, 4, and 5 has the same chance to be generated. If we do this many times and count how many times 1 or 2 or 3 or 4 or 5 have been generated, the counts should be very similar. This is called a uniform distribution, which means that no number has a higher chance of being chosen than another number.

© Yu Zhang, Mathias Funk 2021
Y. Zhang and M. Funk, *Coding Art*, https://doi.org/10.1007/978-1-4842-6264-1_4

Tips   We can also use `random(n)` as a shortcut for `random(0, n)`.

When our code calls `random(m, n)`, Processing will generate a random number (of type `float`) between m and n according to a uniform distribution. That means every number in-between has the same chance to be chosen. If you know computers a bit, you will be surprised that something like this is actually possible. Why? Because computers are known for doing exactly what they have been instructed to do. They just don't invent stuff like random numbers. In fact, the computer follows a complex algorithm to generate "random" numbers. They are not really random, but certainly good enough for our purposes here.

4.1.1 Working with randomness

Why are we using randomness in this book? Because it gives us a very quick and easy source of unpredictable data. That means we give the task of inventing numbers to the computer and also avoid our own bias in choosing only numbers that we like. Randomness can add depth to a rendering because we can create lots of small, subtle changes in visual elements that prevent the entire piece from looking too mathematical. By using randomness, we can also challenge our own creation and find inspiring new looks for the visual elements that we have created so far. Finally, we can use randomness to make choices that are more or less unpredicted and indeed "random."

Let's start with the first one: random values generated by Processing are always of data type `float`, so floating point numbers such as `3.14`, `5.0005`, or `-100.9`. We might need to convert these into integer numbers. Although we could have used the `int` function of Processing, this is often misunderstood (does it "round" or use the next lower or higher integer number?). Therefore, we suggest using `round` as follows:

Generating random numbers

```
// generate random floating point number
float value = random(10, 100);
// convert to integer number
int position = round(value);

// or: the same as above in one step
int position = round(random(10, 100));
```

As mentioned earlier, using the random function in Processing
will generate different numbers every time it is called. Behind this is a
random number generator – think of a tiny machine that creates random
numbers whenever turned on. When Processing creates this "machine"
for a sketch, the generator is initialized in such a way that it will produce
different random numbers for every run of Processing. Sometimes, we
want random numbers that are generated in the same order, giving our
sketch randomness that can be reproduced across different runs. For this
purpose, we can initialize the random number generator with a value that
is always the same.

Generating many random numbers in a loop

```
randomSeed(0);
noStroke();
for(int i = 0; i < 50; i += 5) {
    fill(random(0, 255));
    rect(i, 10, 4, 4);
}
```

In the preceding code, the function randomSeed initializes the generator, and if we run the program multiple times, we see always the same grayscale pattern although we use the random function. Why would we want that? We could, for instance, use different random seeds to generate different artworks and save them together with the random seed. So, when we select best, we have a chance to recreate it with the matching random seed.

? Think about this

Try to change the value in randomSeed or try to move random out of the for loop to see what will happen.

Back to the different types of randomness. When we use the Processing random function, we create uniformly distributed random values. There is also the function randomGaussian which creates random values that are distributed differently. Before all values have the same chance to be chosen with random, now they follow a bell curve or Gaussian distribution with randomGaussian. What is a Gaussian distribution? Let's quickly draw one of the transparent dots with Processing and randomGaussian:

Generating random numbers (Gaussian distribution)

```
noStroke();
fill(80, 40);
// draw a lot of randomly positioned dots
for(int i = 0; i < 20000; i++) {
    // move by 50 pixels to the right, scale by factor 10
    float position = 50 + randomGaussian() * 10;
    rect(position, i % 100, 1, 1);
}
```

? Think about this

Try to use `random` instead of `randomGaussian` and see the difference between both types of randomness. Try changing the value 50 and 10 in `float position = 50 + randomGaussian()*10` to see what will happen.

What you see is that the dots are very crowded in the center of the canvas and get less and less toward both sides of the center line. Now you understand why `randomGaussian` produces a distribution that is nonuniform: values around the center line have a much higher chance to be generated than other values. `randomGaussian` does not take any parameters and will generate values with a mean of 0. "Mean of" means the following: if you would add all values from `randomGaussian` up and then divide this sum by the number of values, you would get 0 as a result (the mean). So, what does that really mean? All values returned by `randomGaussian` are clustered closely around 0; the more the values differ from 0, the less common they become. To practically use this in your code, you might need to use the `map` function on the output of the `randomGaussian` function, so you can spread the values farther away from 0. In the following, we change the first code to use the `map` function:

Using the `map` function on the output of the `randomGaussian` function

```
noStroke();
fill(80, 40);
// draw a lot of randomly positioned dots
```

91

```
for(int i = 0; i < 20000; i++) {
    // map from range [-5, 5] to range [0, width]
    float position = map(randomGaussian(), -5, 5, 0, width);
    rect(position, i % 100, 1, 1);
}
```

In summary, we have seen two types of randomness so far, and both have their own use cases. random is good for randomly filling a limited space or drawing with values that have all the same chance of being generated. It is good for replacing a few values in a sketch to try out new ways of drawing visual elements. The randomGaussian function is good for creating small-scale variations around a value that we have chosen before. Let's try that in a first interactive example to draw with a randomized brush on the canvas:

Draw with a randomized brush on the canvas

```
void setup() {
    size(400, 400);
    background(255);
}
void draw() {
    // move to draw around the mouse position
    translate(mouseX, mouseY);
    // change the color randomly
    stroke(random(0, 200), 10, 50);
    // draw a vertical line from random x-position
    // to another random x-position
    line(randomGaussian(), -10, randomGaussian(), 10);
}
```

? Think about this

In this piece of code, try replacing `randomGaussian` with `random` when drawing a `line` to see what the difference is.

The example shows an empty canvas at first, and we can draw with a random brush directed by the mouse position. The preceding code uses the two different kinds of randomness, `random` for choosing the color and `randomGaussian` for the positioning of lines (i.e., their end points). The color choice is more diverse with `random`, and the line drawing is nicely homogeneous with two close random values generated by `randomGaussian`. Looks like a colorful, quirky fence in the countryside.

4.1.2 Controlling randomness

In the previous section, we have used randomness in different forms to create variation in positioning, movement, or color. We have used randomness in these cases directly, without much filtering and little mapping. This section is about controlling the output of random functions, how we can make creative use of randomness without letting our work look essentially random. Let's start with another color brush that paints colorful blobs with the mouse.

Color brush that paints colorful blobs with the mouse

```
void setup() {
  size(400, 400); background(0); noStroke();
  // change color mode from RGB to HSB
  colorMode(HSB);
}
```

```
void draw() {
  // blur previous output
  filter(BLUR, 1);
  // mouse is pressed, draw color blobs
  if (mousePressed) {
    // move drawing position to mouse position
    translate(mouseX, mouseY);
    // draw 5 blobs per frame
    for(int i = 0; i < 5; i++) {
      // choose HSB color with random hue
      fill(random(0, 255), 255, 255);
      // generate random position around mouse position
      PVector pos = new PVector(random(-20, 20),random(-20, 20));
      // calculate blob size based distance from mouse position
      // (we used translate before, mouse position is now (0, 0))
      float size = 20 - dist(0, 0, pos.x, pos.y);
      // draw blob
      ellipse(pos.x, pos.y, size, size);
    }
  }
}
```

Tips   If you define colorMode as HSB in setup or anywhere else in your code, the values in fill are corresponding to hue–saturation–brightness. You can always switch the color mode, which might be helpful to adjust colors differently.

This code first sets the canvas size and properties as you might have seen many times before, but then we switch the colorMode from RGB to HSB. That means when we specify color values in the remainder of the code, the three values that fill, stroke, and other calls take mean something else. With the HSB color mode, the three values do not encode the color channels red, green, and blue anymore, but instead specify hue, saturation, and brightness. Note that the values are still in the range 0–255. This allows us to create colors differently: we can, for instance, take a hue that is yellow, and, by playing with saturation and brightness, we can create many different shades of this yellow easily. Once again, if you use fill or stroke with the HSB model, you are using it like this: fill(hue, saturation, brightness) and stroke(hue, saturation, brightness). Think of a color wheel with all the rainbow colors: the hue selects a point on the wheel, like Goethe's color theory and his color wheels.

Saturation determines how strong or weak the color is, and brightness specifies how bright it is. In the preceding example, we use colors with randomly selected hues and full saturation and brightness to create vibrant color blobs on the black background.

In every frame, when the mouse is pressed, we draw five blobs with random color hue, position, and size. The position is determined with a random point around the mouse pointer. The size depends on the blob's distance to the mouse pointer. The farther it is away from the mouse pointer, the smaller it is rendered. We achieve this by simply subtracting the distance from 20. We could have mapped this differently using Processing's map function.

Back to controlling randomness. What if we want to limit the selection of random colors and tie it to the direction of the blob compared to the mouse pointer? Let's try with this replacement of the previous draw function (Figure 4-1):

Tie the range of colors to the direction of mouse movement

```
void draw() {
  // blur previously drawn canvas
  filter(BLUR, 1);
  // mouse is pressed, draw color blobs
  if (mousePressed) {
    // create two points for center and mouse position
    PVector center = new PVector(width/2, height/2);
    PVector mouse = new PVector(mouseX, mouseY);
    // calculate angle between center and mouse in radians
    float angle = PVector.sub(mouse, center).heading();
    // convert from radians to degrees in range [-180, 180]
    angle = degrees(angle);
    // convert from degrees to a hue value in range [0, 255]
    float hue = map(angle, -180, 180, 0, 255);
    // move drawing position to mouse position
    translate(mouseX, mouseY);
    // draw 5 blobs per frame
    for(int i = 0; i < 5; i++) {
      // choose HSB color with random hue
      fill(random(hue - 20, hue + 20) % 255, 255, 255);
      // generate random position around mouse position
      PVector pos = new PVector(random(-20, 20),
      random(-20, 20));
      // calculate blob size based distance from mouse
      // position
      float size = 20 - dist(0, 0, pos.x, pos.y);
```

```
    // draw blob
    ellipse(pos.x, pos.y, size, size);
  }
 }
}
```

The result of this code is a variant of the previous sketch that gives more control of the colors, following a color wheel around the center point of the canvas. To make this happen, we have to first calculate the direction of the mouse position relative to the center point of the canvas. So, by moving the mouse in a circle around the canvas center, we can go through 360 degrees (or rather from -180 to 180). We map the degrees to a hue value in the range 0–255, which we can use in the for loop to draw the individual blobs in slightly different colors. We constrain the random function to hue ±20 and apply the modulo % operator to wrap values larger than 255 around. This only works in the HSB color model, because the hue is like a color wheel wrapping around, so there is no gap or jump at the end of the spectrum: 255 and 0 are directly neighboring hues.

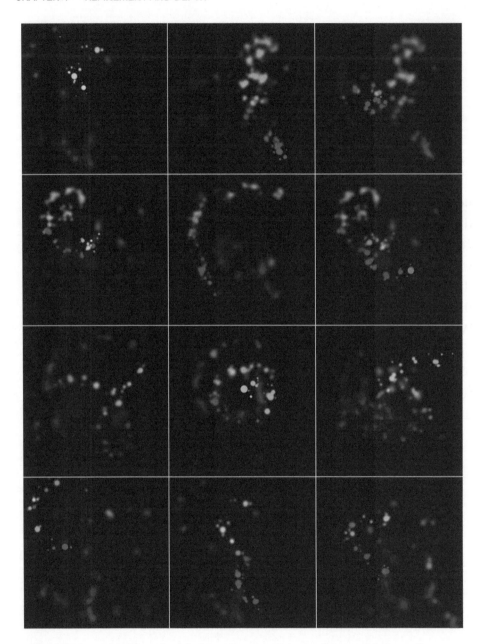

Figure 4-1. *Tie the color palette for randomly drawn blob to the mouse movement*

You can use randomness or simply the distance of different points in the sketch to further tailor the brush in the example. For example, what if we wanted to link the color saturation to the distance of the mouse to the center point.

Tie color saturation to the distance of mouse position to center

```
// BEFORE: choose HSB color with random hue
fill(random(hue - 20, hue + 20) % 255, 255, 255);

// AFTER: choose HSB color with random hue
// and distance -based saturation, constrained to range 0 .. 255
float saturation = constrain(255 - center.dist(mouse), 0, 255);
fill(random(hue - 20, hue + 20) % 255, saturation, 255);
```

? Think about this

Think about why the map function would not really help here.

In this example, we subtract the distance of center point and mouse position from 255, so the highest saturation values are given in mouse locations close to the center point. We also see a new Processing function: constrain.

This function allows us to lock the output into a particular range. We use this in the example to ensure that saturation will not be less than 0, which would naturally happen when the mouse is farther than 255 pixels away from the center. So, we use constrain to lock saturation into the right range for the color saturation: 0..255. When we press and drag the mouse around the center of the canvas, we see that the most vibrant colors are generated in the center and the colors blend gradually to white toward the edges of the canvas.

99

Tips   Try to link distance to brightness instead of saturation and use a different mapping for saturation, for example, the mouse speed. Hint: Use pmouseX and pmouseY for the previous mouse position.

4.1.3 Selecting and making choices with randomness

Finishing the extended section about randomness, we will use randomness to make choices and do things at a random selected time. What does that mean? For example, imagine you have a carefully designed color palette of 20 different colors that match each other well. When painting with the randomized brush as in the examples before, you want to use this color palette, not completely random colors. This means you want to use random colors, but limited to your designed color palette. Let's try a simple example of this idea:

Use random colors with a limited color palette

```
void draw() {
  // color palette as array of type color
  // remember that colors are in HSB mode
  color[] palette = {
    color(160, 255, 255),
    color(220, 200, 200),
    color(120, 200, 200),
    color(120, 0, 220),
    color(220)
  };
  // blur previous output
  filter(BLUR, 1);
```

```
// mouse is pressed, draw color blobs
if (mousePressed) {
  // move drawing position to mouse position
  translate(mouseX, mouseY);
  // draw 5 blobs per frame
  for(int i = 0; i < 5; i++) {
    // choose color randomly from palette array
    int paletteChoice = int(random(0, palette.length));
    fill(palette[paletteChoice]);
    // generate random position around mouse position
    PVector pos = new PVector(random(-20, 20), random(-20, 20));
    // calc. blob size based distance from mouse
    float size = 20 - pos.dist(new PVector());
    // draw blob
    ellipse(pos.x, pos.y, size, size);
  }
 }
}
```

This example shows how to first define a color palette with an array of colors. We use the Processing color data type for this array. When we draw, we select random colors from this palette, which means we have to pick an element from the palette array. We generate a random integer number ranging from 0 till palette.length - 1, which is then used to retrieve the random color from the palette array.

We know already how to use random to generate numbers in a given range. We just need to convert these numbers to the integer format before we can use them to address the different cells of an array. Why? Because array positions are always whole numbers. There is no array element 9.75, right? In the preceding code, we do these steps in two lines of code and then proceed to draw the blobs as before.

? Think about this

Why these numbers? Because array indexing works with zero-based numbering. The first element is at position 0, then second at position 1, and so on. This means that the last element of an array is at position `length-1`.

We can also use randomness to make choices, for instance, choosing between drawing a red or blue rectangle or drawing a rectangle or circle. As a simple example of such a choice, consider the following code:

Using randomness to make choices

```
if(random(0, 100) < 70) {
    // do this in 70% of all cases
} else {
    // do this in the remaining 30% of cases
}
```

This code uses the random function to generate a random number between 0 and 100. If this number is smaller than 70, then we execute the first code block. If the number is 70 or higher, we execute the else code block. With random, every number has the same chance of being generated; therefore, the first block is executed in 70% of all cases and the second one in 30% of cases (70% and 30% add up to 100%).

In our next example, we turn the 70 into an interactive value that depends on the mouse pointer. The example shows 100 shapes in red or blue. For every shape, depending on the mouse position, we make a choice between red and blue fill color (horizontal direction) and whether the shape is a square or a circle (vertical direction).

Using interactive values that depend on the mouse pointer

```
PVector[] positions = new PVector[100];
void setup() {
  size(400, 400); noStroke(); rectMode(CENTER);
  // initialize 100 random positions
  for (int i = 0; i < 100; i++) {
    positions[i] = new PVector(random(width), random(height));
  }
}
// empty draw because all drawing is done in mouseMoved
// (this empty draw is still needed otherwise the program
// stops)
void draw() { }
// we draw when the mouse has moved
void mouseMoved() {
  background(0);
  // loop through all positions
  for (PVector position : positions) {
    // red fill color if random value is
    // smaller than horizontal mouse position
    if (random(0, width) < mouseX) {
      fill(255, 0, 0);
    } else {
      fill(0, 0, 255);
    }
    // draw rectangle if random value is
    // smaller than vertical mouse position
```

```
    if (random(0, height) < mouseY) {
      rect(position.x, position.y, 10, 10);
    } else {
      ellipse(position.x, position.y, 10, 10);
    }
  }
}
```

? Think about this

Think about how you could use randomness. Would it be about choosing colors, shaping some visual elements, or about deciding which elements to show at a time? Read on to see what else we can do with randomness.

When you move the mouse across the canvas and stop from time to time, you will see that the distribution (or proportion) of red vs. blue and rectangles vs. circles changes. The most extreme distributions can be observed when you move the mouse pointer to the corners of the canvas. For instance, in the top-left corner, you will see close to 100% blue circles, whereas you will get almost 100% red rectangles in the opposite corner.

4.1.4 Working with noise

Normal randomness can be quite jumpy with random and with the randomGaussian function. What if we want randomness that moves smoothly between values, instead of jumping wildly in the given range? We can use noise, which produces random values that follow a smooth curve. Let's see a quick comparison between Processing's random and the noise function.

Using the `noise` function

```
void setup() {
  size(400, 200); background(255); noStroke();
}
void draw() {
  // first the 'random' generated position
  fill(255, 0, 255, 100);
  rect(frameCount, random(0, height), 5, 5);
  // second the 'noise' generated position
  fill(255, 0, 0, 100);
  ellipse(frameCount, map(noise(frameCount/100.), 0, 1, 0,
  height), 5, 5);
}
```

This kind of noise is called Perlin noise and allows to create smoother transitions than working with random values. To use noise, we have to send different parameters than with random. We use values between 0 and 1. The noise function produces values between 0 and 1, and using the same input value will produce the same noise output value. To get a sequence of values, we have to move through the noise slowly, like in the following example.

Reminder   Try to find out more about "Perlin noise" online. There is a story behind it, and you might find more interesting computer graphics material to dive into.

This example (Figure 4-2) renders 40 rectangles (width divided by 10) that are colored and sized based on the noise function. With a BLUR filter, this results in a fog or fire-like visual effect. The rectangles are spaced horizontally by 10 pixels and move down 1 pixel per frame (using frameCount). With the modulo operator (%), we ensure that the rectangles start again at the top after leaving the canvas at the bottom. We use a grayscale fill color that ranges from 0 to 255. Note that we use the noise function for the color depending on both i and frameCount. This ensures that the noise value changes across the 40 rectangles (horizontal) and also over time (vertical). We use very small steps to move through the noise, for instance, frameCount/100.. You can try and experiment with the step size to speed up the changes.

Use the noise function for smoother transitions

```
void setup() {
  size(400, 400); noStroke(); background(0);
}
void draw() {
  // add blur effect
  filter(BLUR, 1);
  // draw rectangles over entire canvas width spaced by
  // 10 pixels
  for(int i = 0; i < width; i += 10) {
    // multiply noise output in range [0..1] with 255
    // because 255 is the largest color value
    fill(noise(i/10. + frameCount/100.) * 255);
    // multiply noise output in range [0..1] with 15
    // because we want 15 pixels max size for rectangles
    float size = noise(0.3 + frameCount/1000.) * 15;
    rect(i, frameCount % height, size, size);
  }
}
```

Tips   Try to use different colors or even a color palette. You can give the visual effect some real fire.

The previous examples show that we can use random numbers like any other numbers, and there is an endless supply of such data. It does not matter whether we generate random numbers to try out variants of visual elements or to get new ideas. The basic ideas are always the same: think about the range (from ... to ...) and distribution (uniform or Gaussian, etc.) before using the values in your code. Play with the outcome and then refine the use of randomness until you are satisfied with the outcome.

This section is all about randomness and noise, which is essentially an unlimited data source that we can use as much as we want in our sketches. Of course, you have to think carefully how and where to use random values, whether to filter and scale it, and where you need to precisely determine the data in your sketches. In the next section, we will learn how to use historical data.

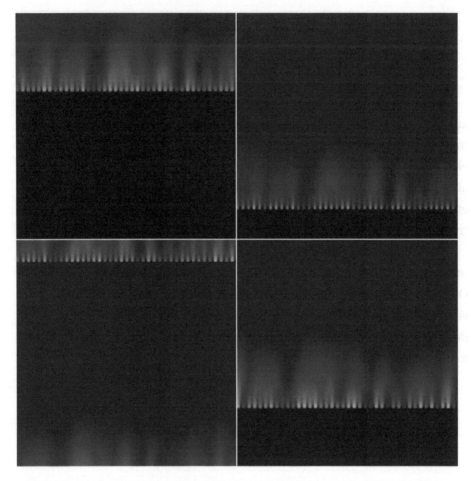

Figure 4-2. *Forty rectangles that are shaded gray and sized based on the* noise *function. The "fire" effect is mainly caused by the BLUR filter*

4.2 MemoryDot

In the past sections, we have worked mostly with random or computed data that is not directly influenced by user interactions. Although many examples use the mouse position, we creatively hide the fact that such input can be quite jumpy and erratic at times. This section is about smoothing data and creating smooth transitions between different settings.

Also, we will work with a structure that we actually don't need to understand to use it. This structure is the MemoryDot which is an extension of our trusty helper, the PVector. It implements a point and also keeps a memory of previous locations.

Before this chapter, we had to fully grasp how our structures work; now we will work with the MemoryDot and trust that it works in all our use cases. In other words, we will treat this structure as a black box and only use its interfaces to work with its internal (hidden) functions. Sounds exciting, right? Let's go!

4.2.1 Smoothing

As a starting point for this section, we will draw a single bright blue dot around the mouse position. The dot follows the mouse position very accurately, with only minimal delay. If you move the mouse out of the canvas and enter the canvas at a different edge, the dot will jump onto this new position instantly.

Draw a single bright blue dot around the mouse position

```
void setup() {
  size(400, 400); noStroke(); colorMode(HSB);
  background(0);
}
void draw() {
  filter(BLUR, 1);
  // paint a bright blue dot
  fill(170, 255, 255);
  // at mouse position
  PVector m = new PVector(mouseX, mouseY);
  ellipse(m.x, m.y, 28, 28);
}
```

What if we want to let the dot follow the mouse position with a bit of delay and slightly smoother movements? We can use the class MemoryDot as a replacement for PVector m.

Use MemoryDot for delay and slightly smoother movements

```
MemoryDot m;
void setup() {
  size(400, 400); noStroke(); colorMode(HSB);
  background(0);
  m = new MemoryDot(30);
}
void draw() {
  filter(BLUR, 1);
  // paint a bright blue dot
  fill(170, 255, 255);
  // update memory dot with current mouse position
  m.update(mouseX, mouseY);
  // draw at position given by memory dot
  ellipse(m.x, m.y, 28, 28);
}
```

This preceding code will not work directly; we still need to add the MemoryDot class into the code folder. How to do that and use another code file next to your sketch? Click the small triangle next to the sketch name and select "new tab." Type a new name such as "MemoryDot," and then copy and paste the code into the file in the new tab.

Code for the MemoryDot class

```
class MemoryDot extends PVector {
  PVector[] internal; float x, y, energy;
  public MemoryDot(int size) {
    internal = new PVector[size]; x = 0; y = 0;
  }
  public void update(float x, float y) {
    update(new PVector(x, y));
  }
  public void update(PVector newValue) {
    float x = 0; float y = 0; this.energy = 0;
    for (int i = internal.length -1; i > 0; i--) {
      if (internal[i] != null) {
        x += internal[i].x/float(internal.length);
        y += internal[i].y/float(internal.length);
      }
      if (internal[i] != null && internal[i-1] != null) {
        energy += internal[i-1].dist(internal[i])/
        float(internal.length);
      }
      internal[i] = internal[i-1];
    }
    internal[0] = newValue;
    if (internal[0] != null) {
      x += internal[0].x/float(internal.length);
      y += internal[0].y/float(internal.length);
    }
    this.x = x; this.y = y;
  }
}
```

Reminder   Perhaps you find that the code for MemoryDot looks quite complex and a little hard to understand. Good news: you don't need to fully go through it to be able to use it effectively. It's a bit like the internal Processing functions: we use them all the time, but don't really need to understand how they work internally. (Technical detail: The MemoryDot class is built on top of PVector using its internal mechanisms. We call it MemoryDot because it implements a point (or dot) and also keeps a memory of previous locations.)

If you use MemoryDot in your sketch, you will see that the blue dot now moves differently. It does not make rapid jumps anymore, but steadily gravitates toward the mouse position.

What does the MemoryDot actually do? Whenever you call the update function of a MemoryDot, it stores the updated position in its internal memory. The length of this memory (so how many positions can be stored) is given by the number 30 in new MemoryDot(30).

Now we have all the tools in place to render multiple dots that are gradually bigger and slower moving. Please make sure that you have the MemoryDot file present for the coming two examples as well.

In the first example (Figure 4-3), we have simply created two more MemoryDot objects in the first line and initialized them with different memory lengths: 60 and 90. This means that the m, l, and xl dots will remember gradually more past positions and then also react slower to changes in the current position. Why? Because the MemoryDot will take the average over all positions in memory and then use this average as the new current position of the MemoryDot. In other words, the more positions we remember, the more "old" positions influence the newly incoming positions. It takes more time until this "old" stuff is flushed out. That's why MemoryDot will react slower to position changes with larger memory.

Using the update function of MemoryDot

```
MemoryDot m, l, xl;
void setup() {
  size(400, 400); noStroke(); colorMode(HSB);
  background(0);
  m = new MemoryDot(30);
  l = new MemoryDot(60);
  xl = new MemoryDot(90);
}
void draw() {
  filter(BLUR, 1);
  // update memory dot with current mouse position
  xl.update(mouseX, mouseY);
  // set color of first blue dot
  fill(170, 120, 255);
  // draw at position given by memory dot
  ellipse(xl.x, xl.y, 84, 84);
  // paint smaller but more saturated blue dot
  l.update(mouseX, mouseY);
  fill(170, 160, 255);
```

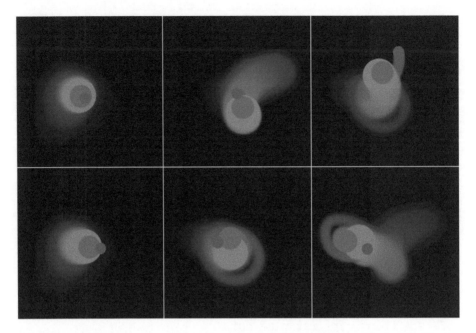

Figure 4-3. *Overlapping circles positioned by different MemoryDot objects. Lightest circle is moving slowest, while darker circles are gradually moving faster toward the mouse position*

```
  ellipse(l.x, l.y, 56, 56);
  // paint smaller but more saturated blue dot
  m.update(mouseX, mouseY);
  fill(170, 200, 255);
  ellipse(m.x, m.y, 28, 28);
}
```

? Think about this

Try to find out about the range of energy and adjust the brightness parameter of fill to have a slower transition between dark and bright.

There is another feature that we can use in our code: energy. Let's try the second example.

Control the brightness with the energy property of MemoryDot

```
void draw() {
  filter(BLUR, 1);
  // paint first blue dot
  fill(170, 120, 100 + xl.energy * 200);
  // update memory dot with current mouse position
  xl.update(mouseX, mouseY);
  // draw at position given by memory dot
  ellipse(xl.x, xl.y, 84, 84);
  // paint other blue dots
  fill(170, 160, 100 + l.energy * 200);
  l.update(mouseX, mouseY);
  ellipse(l.x, l.y, 56, 56);
  fill(170, 200, 100 + m.energy * 50);
  m.update(mouseX, mouseY);
  ellipse(m.x, m.y, 28, 28);
}
```

In this code, we have replaced the fixed brightness value of 255 with 100 + m.energy * 200 which depends on the MemoryDot m's energy. The energy describes how much the past positions differ from each other. That means if the past positions are very different from each other, the energy is high. If they are mostly very close to each other, the energy is low. This is quite visible in the example, because the color turns darker when the dots move slower. You can also see the difference between the dots in how long their memory is and how that influences the energy for each of them.

115

We have now used an existing structure that was built as an extension of Processing's PVector class. We did not need to understand how MemoryDot works precisely; we can use it in our sketches as a black box. Once we know how it behaves, we can use it in many other places (as you will see later in this book).

4.2.2 Smoothly working with many things

Reminder   How to add MemoryDot next to your sketch? Click the small triangle next to the sketch name, and select "new tab." Type "MemoryDot," and paste the MemoryDot code into the new tab. The code is provided earlier, or just use the Processing library for this book.

We have seen earlier how we can use multiple MemoryDot objects together. This is scalable to many things, but we always need to think about what kind of effect we want to achieve. The following example is more complex: we will use noise, random, and also MemoryDot to animate a field of artificial grass and a purple surprise.

The coming example (Figure 4-4) starts relatively short and will grow a bit in the next few pages. Let's dive in: first of all, we use 10000 positions to represent grass blades in 3D space. The grass blades are randomly positioned with their x, y coordinates on a plane. The random positions are generated in the setup function. The z coordinate of every grass blade determines its vertical length. Grass blades are drawn as lines with a fixed lower point on the plane and a movable upper point that responds to several influences.

Draw a field of artificial grass

```
// Note: This example need the MemoryDot class as shown above.
// Before running this code, add the MemoryDot class as an
// additional tab to Processing.

// 10000 grass blades to render
PVector[] positions = new PVector[10000];

// memorydot for smoothly changing the wind direction
MemoryDot windDirection = new MemoryDot(250);

// wind target will be updated regularly
PVector windTarget = new PVector(random(-20, 20), random(-20, 20));

void setup() {
  size(400, 400, P3D);
  colorMode(HSB);
```

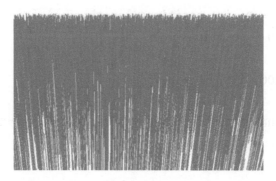

Figure 4-4. Example of using 10000 positions (representing grass blades in 3D space) to draw field of artificial grass

```
  // initialize random positions for grass blades,
  // x, y are position, z represents grass blade length
  for (int i = 0; i < positions.length; i++) {
    positions[i] = new PVector(random(-250, 600),
    random(100, 600), random(90, 100));
  }
}

void draw() {
  // white background in HSB model
  background(255, 0, 255);
  // translate and rotate for good viewing angle
  translate(0, 0, -300);
  rotateX(radians(-15));

  // every 150 frames, reset the wind target
  if (frameCount % 150 == 0) {
    windTarget = new PVector(random(-5, 5), random(-5, 5));
  }
  // update wind direction with current target
  windDirection.update(windTarget);

  // draw grass at all positions one by one
  for (int i = 0; i < positions.length; i++) {
    PVector p = positions[i];
    // set green stroke color
    stroke(100, 150, 50 + p.z);
    // use noise for wind strength
    float windStrength = noise(frameCount/500.) * 2;
    // draw every grass blade
```

```
   line(p.x, 200, p.y, p.x - windDirection.x * windStrength,
     200 - p.z, p.y - windDirection.y * windStrength);
  }
}
```

Although this example is not complete yet, you can try it out and see the green grass flow in a 3D space. What makes the grass flow? We use simulated "wind" that blows over the plane and moves the tips of the grass blades in one or another direction over time. This is the point where we use a MemoryDot object to smoothly change the direction of the wind. We initialize this MemoryDot in the beginning of the code example and set a new random wind target position every 150 frames. The wind target is randomly generated in a small range, because we want the tips of the grass blades to move naturally. The wind target is used to update the MemoryDot `windDirection`. This smoothly moves the wind direction toward the target until the next wind target will be set. When drawing the grass blade, we modulate the wind direction a little bit with `noise`, which results in different "gusts" of wind in the current wind direction. Otherwise, all blades would move, and we would lose the more organic look. We will continue this example in the next section.

4.3 Using computed values

This section is meant to give structure to what we have used a lot in the past sections and examples: expressions calculating values. Think about the expression `p.x + windDirection.x * windStrength` from the previous example. Although the variables are named ok, this is hard to understand without knowing about the wind simulation. When these expressions become longer and they are used in more than one place in the code, it is better to extract them into a function – as we will see in the next part.

4.3.1 Computing values with functions

Functions allow to replace expressions that are complex or used in many places in the code and give them their own place and parameters, so the rest of the code can be simplified. There are other reasons for using functions, but this will suffice for now. We have been using functions since the beginning of this book. All functionality that Processing provides us with, from fill to rect and ellipse to the functions of the PVector class, they all are functions defined to be used and reused.

We will now change the previous example without changing how it looks or works:

Continued example for the animated field of grass

```
// beginning and setup as before
void draw() {
  // white background in HSB model
  background(255, 0, 255);
  // translate and rotate for good viewing angle
  translate(0, 0, -300);
  rotateX(radians(-15));

  // every 150 frames, reset the wind target
  if (frameCount % 150 == 0) {
    windTarget = new PVector(random(-5, 5), random(-5, 5));
  }
  // update wind direction with current target
  windDirection.update(windTarget);

  // draw grass at all positions one by one
  for (int i = 0; i < positions.length; i++) {
    PVector p = positions[i];
```

```
    // set green stroke color
    stroke(100, 150, 50 + p.z);
    // get grass blade tip with new function
    PVector ptip = getGrassTip(p, i);
    // draw every grass blade between p and ptip
    line(p.x, 200, p.y, ptip.x, ptip.z, ptip.y);
  }
}
// new function just for getting the tip of a grass blade
PVector getGrassTip(PVector grassBladePosition, int i) {
    // copy position and add wind
    PVector grassBladeTip = grassBladePosition.copy();
    // use noise for wind strength
    float windStrength = noise(frameCount/500.) * 2;
    grassBladeTip.x += windDirection.x * windStrength;
    grassBladeTip.y += windDirection.y * windStrength;
    grassBladeTip.z = 200 - grassBladePosition.z;
    // return the position of the grass blade tip
    return grassBladeTip;
}
```

What happened in this example? We replaced the complex expressions
that were used to compute the position of the grass blade tip into a new
function getGrassTip at the end of the code example. This new function
receives the original position of a grass blade (grassBladePosition),
copies it (grassBladeTip), and adds the influence of the wind for this
position. Then the copy is returned (see the return keyword). Now look up
and check how this new function is used in the draw function: we call it to
compute the grass blade tip position ptip for every grass blade position.
Then the drawing of the line is getting really simple, just a line between
two points p and ptip.

Now that the code is simplified and better structured, we can add more nuance to the movement of the grass blade tips. We use individual deviations per grass blade that are calculated with the noise function, bx, by. These deviations are quite small and create an organic feel of the entire field.

Continued example: let grass blades move more organically

```
PVector getGrassTip(PVector grassBladePosition, int i) {
    // copy position and add wind
    PVector grassBladeTip = grassBladePosition.copy();
    // use noise for wind strength
    float windStrength = noise(frameCount/500.) * 2;
    // use noise for individual deviations of grass blades
    float devX = -10 + noise(i/100. + frameCount/100., i/130.)
    * 20;
    float devY = -10 + noise(i/170. + frameCount/200., i/100.)
    * 20;
    grassBladeTip.x += windDirection.x * windStrength - devX;
    grassBladeTip.y += windDirection.y * windStrength - devY;
    grassBladeTip.z = 200 - grassBladePosition.z;
    // return the position of the grass blade tip
    return grassBladeTip;
}
```

That's a quick change to the getGrassTip function, and the grass blades move even more organically. We added two new variables devX and devY that introduce individual noise for every grass blade tip. After defining and computing them, we subtract them from the previous grass blade tip position, and done.

Are you ready for the finishing touches (Figure 4-5)? Let's look at the draw function again and add three more things: a more differentiated color per grass blade, a small flower bud for 20% of all grass blades, and finally the big bouncing purple ball that adds a bit of surreal feel to the scene. We have seen how bouncing works in the first chapter. So, this example combines aspects of steps 1, 2, and 3 in a single scene.

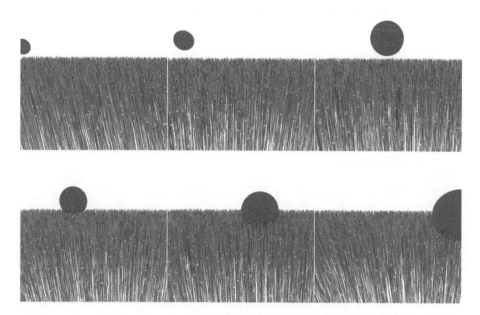

Figure 4-5. *Snapshots of the full grass field example with the large purple ball bouncing through the organically moving grass*

Final step: animate artificial grass and add a purple surprise

```
void draw() {
  // same as before...

  // draw grass at all positions one by one
  for (int i = 0; i < positions.length; i++) {
    PVector p = positions[i];
    // set individual stroke color differently
```

```
stroke(100, 150, 50 + noise(i/100. + frameCount/100.,
i/10. + frameCount/200.) * 150);
// get grass blade tip with new function
PVector ptip = getGrassTip(p, i);
// draw every grass blade
line(p.x, 200, p.y, ptip.x, ptip.z, ptip.y);
// every fifth grass blade gets a flower
if (i % 5 == 0) {
  pushMatrix();
  translate(ptip.x, ptip.z, ptip.y);
  fill(190, 255, 200, 40); noStroke();
  ellipse(0, 0, 2, 2);
  popMatrix();
  }
}

// draw the crazy purple bouncing sphere
fill(200, 255, 255); noStroke();
translate(-500 + frameCount % 1000, 100 -
abs(sin(frameCount/40.) * 80), -500 + frameCount % 1000);
sphere(60);
}
```

In this final example, we added and changed three things: The stroke is now controlled partly by the noise function, which in turn is depending on the frameCount. Second, we added a flower bud decoration for every fifth grass blade, which basically uses the the ptip position to draw an ellipse like a halo around the tip of the grass blade. Finally, we added the bouncing sphere below the for loop, which uses several functions that we have seen before to diagonally bounce through the grass. Fun times!

The most important point of this section is that we critically look at our code and simplify it to be able to move forward with even more complexity. The process of extracting code and moving it into a function is professionally also called refactoring, and it is a common way to simplify the structure of code. We introduce it here explicitly, because we need it in the next few sections where we will either refactor or construct functions from scratch to compute data for us.

4.3.2 Interpolation

Interpolation means finding a value between two given values. Imagine someone gives you two colors and asks for an intermediate color in the middle or at 30% or 80%. Interpolation can give you these colors very precisely. Luckily, Processing has two functions for exactly that, lerp and lerpColor, which are super easy to use. Let's look at an example that interpolates position and color between two moving balls of different colors. Again, we use PVector to store the position of the balls and the z coordinate for the color. Can we actually store a color in the z coordinate, which is a normally number? This little trick works because Processing treats all colors as numbers.

? Think about this

Look at the two functions lerp and lerpColor on the Processing reference page to understand values inside these functions. It is important to understand how the interpolation works: the first two parameters are the start and end value of the interpolation range, and the third parameter determines where in the space between start (0) and end (1) the resulting value is. This is quite related to the map function. Can you think why? See the following for an explanation.

Using the `lerp` and `lerpColor` functions

```
PVector left = new PVector(50, 0, color(0, 255, 255));
PVector right = new PVector(350, 0, color(0, 255, 255));
void setup() {
  size(400, 200); noStroke(); colorMode(HSB);
}
void draw() {
  background(0);
  // move two balls vertically up and down
  left.y = map(sin(frameCount/100.), -1, 1, 20, height-20);
  right.y = map(cos(frameCount/200.), -1, 1, 20, height-20);
  // draw two balls: first left, then right
  fill((color) left.z);
  ellipse(left.x, left.y, 20, 20);
  fill((color) right.z);
  ellipse(right.x, right.y, 20, 20);
  // calculate current interpolation
  float ip = (frameCount % 500)/500.;
  // interpolate between left and right position
  PVector currentPosition = PVector.lerp(left, right, ip);
  // interpolate between left and right color
  fill(lerpColor((color) left.z, (color) right.z, ip));
  // draw middle ball
  ellipse(currentPosition.x, currentPosition.y, 20, 20);
  // extra effect: reset colors if interpolation is 0
  if (ip == 0) {
    left.z = color(random(0, 160), 255, 255);
    right.z = color(random(120, 255), 255, 255);
  }
}
```

Reminder   You might think that we don't need to use `lerpColor` because the position interpolation with `lerp` also interpolates the z coordinate. This does not work because the interpolation of colors is more complex than between simple numbers: try searching for color spaces online and compare the direct path between colors in a color space with the result of using `lerpColor`. Do you see the difference?

The fundamental point to understand about interpolation is that an interpolation operation needs two values (colors, positions, or numbers) that mark the start and the end of a range. Next to that, we need an interpolation amount that determines the point in the space between the values that we are interested in. The interpolation amount ranges from 0 to 1. An interpolation amount closer to 0 indicates that we are interested in a value closer to the first value, and an interpolation amount closer to 1 maps to a value closer to second value. The interpolation amount 0.5 gives us exactly the middle value between the first and the second values. In the preceding example, we use `lerp` to interpolate a position for the middle ball between the left and the right balls. We use `lerpColor` to interpolate a color for the middle balls between the left and right ball. The interpolation amount is following the `frameCount`.

You might ask, is interpolation about the average? Yes, but the average (or mean) usually refers to the exact middle point, which you can get with interpolation amount `0.5`. Interpolation can do more: it can give you all other possible positions between the two values. The example shows this clearly, as we see a smooth animation of the middle ball through all positions (and colors) between the left and the right balls.

4.3.3 Interpolation with functions

How to use functions in the interpolation example? So far we have moved the two outer balls and then calculated the middle ball's position. Another way would be to calculate all positions and then paint them in one go. Let's try this with a small change on how the right ball moves. We use the previous example and replace the draw function as follows.

Interpolate balls in position and color

```
void draw() {
  background(0);
  // move two balls vertically
  left.y = getBallYPosition(frameCount);
  right.y = getBallYPosition(frameCount - 1000);
  // draw left and right balls
  drawBall(0, 20);
  drawBall(1, 20);
  // calculate current interpolation
  float ip = (frameCount % 500)/500.;
  // reset colors if interpolation is 0
  if (ip == 0) {
    left.z = color(random(0, 160), 255, 255);
    right.z = color(random(120, 255), 255, 255);
  }
  // draw big middle ball
  right.y = getBallYPosition(frameCount - 1000 * ip);
  drawBall(ip, 20);
}
float getBallYPosition(float time) {
  return map(sin(time/200.), -1, 1, 20, height-20);
}
```

```
void drawBall(float ip, int size) {
  // interpolate between left and right position
  PVector position = PVector.lerp(left, right, ip);
  // interpolate between left and right color
  fill(lerpColor((color) left.z, (color) right.z, ip));
  // draw ball
  ellipse(position.x, position.y, size, size);
}
```

In this example, the middle ball moves from left to right as if it already knows where the right ball will be. As promised earlier, we can do this by introducing a single new function getBallYPosition. This function takes time as input and calculates the vertical position (y position) of a ball at that time. Because we are using a periodic function like sin, this is possible. It would not be possible with user input or a random function. With sin, however, we can calculate the value exactly for any given time, either in the future or in the past. A second function, drawBall, replaces all drawing code for the three balls. We use it to draw the left and right balls by interpolating with the minimum interpolation value 0 and the maximum interpolation value 1. The middle ball is drawn by interpolating dynamically between left and right ball positions and also their colors. Looking at the function drawBall itself, it is quite straightforward: interpolate position and color, and then draw ball accordingly. By restructuring our code like this, we remove a lot of duplicate code.

With the two new functions getBallYPosition and drawBall, it is easier to extend the code again with additional (small) balls. Take the next example, in which we replace only the draw function. We introduce two new variables called steps and stepSize and add a for loop that renders extra small balls in a nice smooth curve between the left and the right balls. The middle ball will travel on this curve from the left to the right ball.

Add intermediate steps in the interpolation example

```
void draw() {
  background(0);
  // set number and size of intermediate steps
  float steps = 50;
  float stepSize = 20;
  // move two balls vertically
  left.y = getBallYPosition(frameCount);
  right.y = getBallYPosition(frameCount - stepSize * steps);
  // draw left and right balls
  drawBall(0, 20);
  drawBall(1, 20);
  // calculate current interpolation
  float ip = (frameCount % 500)/500.;
  // reset colors if interpolation is 0
  if (ip == 0) {
    left.z = color(random(0, 160), 255, 255);
    right.z = color(random(120, 255), 255, 255);
  }
  // go through all intermediate steps
  for (int i = 0; i < steps; i++) {
    right.y = getBallYPosition(frameCount - stepSize * i);
    drawBall(i/steps, 5);
  }
  // draw big middle ball
  right.y = getBallYPosition(frameCount - stepSize * steps * ip);
  drawBall(ip, 20);
}
```

As the last modification, we link the `steps` and `stepSize` variables to the mouse position to add interactivity. Now, `steps` depends on `mouseX`, and `stepSize` depends on `mouseY`. This allows us to play interactively with the number of intermediate balls and how many wiggles they follow. This modification is also the reason why we initially chose the `float` type for `steps` and `stepSize`.

Let the intermediate steps in the example react to the mouse

```
// determine how many steps we want via x mouse position
float steps = (int) map(mouseX, 0, width, 2, 200);
float stepSize = (int) map(mouseY, 0, height, 100, 2);
```

This big example (Figure 4-6) shows in a few steps how we can first simplify the code by introducing computed values and functions. After that, we can use these additional structures to enrich the work. In this case, we moved from pure interpolation to using functions to compute positions and draw all visual elements. Only with this change, we could make the steps toward the many intermediate steps that are drawn in a smooth curve between the left and right balls.

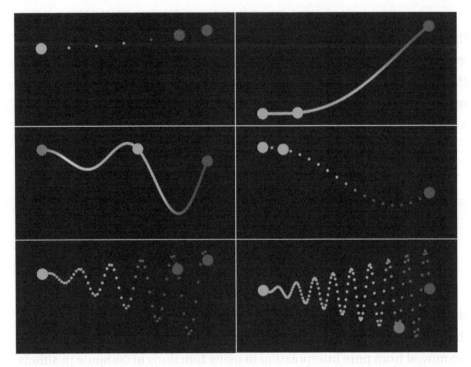

Figure 4-6. *Examples of color and position interpolation for different mouse positions (controlling the number of intermediate steps)*

There are a few practical things to note when making such changes: first, make sure that you always keep a copy of the code before making big changes. Apply the changes one by one and test after each change whether the output is as expected (or better). Try to avoid distractions while structuring code; it is a demanding task that needs your full attention. When you extract code into a function, carefully check the order of parameters in the function – what you fill in, how you use the input inside the function, and how you return and use output of the function in the rest of the program. We will come back to these hints in the final part of this book.

4.4 Interactivity

The final section in this chapter deals with interaction. Now we go beyond our previous use of the mouse to make Processing sketches interactive. For instance, when we use the mouse, we are mostly interested in the mouse position, mouse presses, drags, and clicks. The mouse position provides us with numerical values that we can use to control visual elements or even many things. Mouse presses and clicks provide us with on/off events, a simple transition between the state "mouse is not pressed" to the state "mouse is pressed." These two relatively simple interactions allow controlling complex user interfaces, as you can see in your computer. Even Processing can be controlled almost entirely with the mouse. In short, a very powerful means of interaction.

Still, you might prefer a different way for interaction with your creative work. This section will help understand the fundamental aspects of interactive input and how you can make a transition from the mouse to other input devices such as keyboards, cameras, microphones, and all kinds of simple or complex sensors. Let's start by looking at the mouse and keyboard functions of Processing.

4.4.1 Mouse interaction

We have worked with different mouse functions before in the book. You have seen the `mousePressed` variable that can be used easily in `draw` to switch different visuals according to whether the mouse is pressed or not. We used different mouse handlers as well. Handlers are special built-in functions in Processing that are automatically called when a specific event occurs. For example, there are the `mouseMoved` and `mouseDragged` handlers. The first is called automatically whenever the mouse is moved in any way (but not when a mouse button is pressed). The second handler is called when the mouse is moved with the button pressed, which is usually called "dragging" the mouse. Apart from these functions, we can let Processing

133

notify the sketch when the mouse button is pressed down (mousePressed), when it is released again (mouseReleased), or when both actions happen in quick succession (mouseClicked). The following example shows an example of switching visuals depending on the state of the mouse buttons (without distinguishing between left and right mouse buttons). Only mousePressed exists in a version as a variable or as a handler. All other mouse interaction functions are handlers only.

Different aspects of mouse interaction

```
void setup() {
  size(400, 400);
  background(0); noStroke(); colorMode(HSB);
}
void draw() {
  // only blur canvas if the mouse is not pressed
  filter(BLUR, mousePressed ? 0 : 1);
  // translate to mouse position
  translate(mouseX, mouseY);
  // compute the distance that the mouse
  // has moved this frame
  float size = 5 + dist(pmouseX, pmouseY, mouseX, mouseY);
  // generate sparkles
  for (int i = 0; i < 5; i++) {
    // draw colorful sparkles if mouse is pressed
    if (mousePressed) {
      fill(100 + random(-20, 20), 255, 255, 180);
    } else {
      fill(255, 180);
    }
```

```
    ellipse(size * random(-1, 1), size * random(-1, 1), 2, 2);
  }
}
```

We see two different decision points in the code where different visuals are created depending on the mouse state. The first one happens already at the beginning of the draw function.

mousePressed ? 0 : 1 is a conditional operator, short form of writing if .. else. If mousePressed is true (that means a mouse button is pressed), the filter function receives the input 0. Else, the filter function receives 1. You can use this conditional operator in many ways to make a decision between two values, but be aware that it is sometimes easy to overlook and harder to understand for beginners than a full if .. else control structure.

The second decision point is about the color of the sparkles that are generated around the mouse pointer. As long as the mouse button is not pressed, the sparkles are white. When the mouse is pressed, the sparkles turn greenish. Overall, we see either fading white sparkles or sticky green sparkles in this example.

So far, we have ignored the different mouse buttons entirely. This changes with the next example. Just replace a few lines of code in the previous example and run it.

Generate the color of the sparkles around the mouse pointer

PREVIOUS:

```
    // draw colorful sparkles if mouse is pressed
    if (mousePressed) {
      fill(100 + random(-20, 20), 255, 255, 180);
    } else {
      fill(255, 180);
    }
```

NEW:

```
// draw colorful sparkles if mouse is pressed
// button left --> red, button right --> blue
if (mousePressed && mouseButton == LEFT) {
  fill(240 + random(-20, 20), 255, 255, 180);
} else if (mousePressed && mouseButton == RIGHT) {
  fill(160 + random(-20, 20), 255, 255, 180);
} else {
  fill(255, 180);
}
```

You probably understand most of the preceding example, but there is one new thing here: the && connection between two different parts of the if or else if conditions (mousePressed && mouseButton == LEFT). This connection is called a "logical AND" operation, which returns true only in the case that both expressions (before and after &&) are true. In this example, the fill color will only be changed if the mouse is pressed AND mouseButton is LEFT (or RIGHT in the second condition).

? Think about this

Logical operators allow you to express more complex conditions. Next to the AND operator that we introduced earlier, there is also the "logical OR" operator || which will return true if one of the two expressions or both are true. Try it out.

In this variation of the previous "sparkles" example, we distinguish the left from the right mouse button by checking the mouseButton variable and comparing against LEFT or RIGHT. Now, you will see differently colored sparkles depending on which mouse button you press down when drawing on the canvas.

4.4.2 Keyboard interaction

The keyboard is the second main input for interaction. Unlike the mouse position, keyboard input is more discrete. That means keys will not provide a continuous value, but an event and the key character ("key code"). We can, for instance, work with arrow keys and a variable to precisely position a visual element. In the following example, we use the arrow keys on the keyboard to move the light rectangle around. Any other key will reset the position in the center of the canvas.

Use arrow keys to change precisely positions of visual elements

```
PVector pos;
void setup() {
  size(400, 400);
  noStroke(); rectMode(CENTER);
  // start position: middle center point of canvas
  pos = new PVector(width/2, height/2);
}
void draw() {
  background(0);
  fill(200, 200, 255);
  rect(pos.x, pos.y, 40, 40);
}
void keyPressed() {
  // check if key is special (not letter or number)
  if (key == CODED) {
    // for special keys, check key code
    if (keyCode == UP) { pos.y--; }
    else if (keyCode == DOWN) { pos.y++; }
    else if (keyCode == LEFT) { pos.x--; }
    else if (keyCode == RIGHT) { pos.x++; }
```

```
  } else {
    // all other keys --> reset position
    pos.set(width/2, height/2);
  }
}
```

? Think about this

Try extending this example by checking the SHIFT key to make the rectangle move faster in one direction when pressing SHIFT. What else could you influence with the keyboard?

Precise control is a strength of the keyboard; every key press counts. As we will see in the next example, we can also work with the content of the keys that are pressed. Let's start by simply printing the pressed key as a bold character on the canvas.

This example uses a brief setup and an empty draw function, and most of the action happens in the keyPressed function. In the beginning, we load a font that we previously created with Processing tools. How did we do that? Open Processing and the Tools menu. There is an option "Create font..." that allows to pick a font from your computer, determine the size, and convert it into a format that Processing can use directly. It works better if you specify the right font size already, so the rendered text is sharp in the end. Processing creates a new font file that should be located in the same folder as the Processing sketch.

Print the pressed key as a bold character on the canvas

```
PFont f;
void setup() {
  size(400, 400);
  // load a specific font to print text
  f = loadFont("InterUI-ExtraBold-250.vlw");
  background(0);
}
void draw() {}
void keyPressed() {
  // draw character
  background(0); fill(255);
  // set text rendering options
  textFont(f, 250);
  textSize(250);
  // measure character width
  float charWidth = textWidth(key);
  // draw character centered
  text(key, (width - charWidth) / 2., 300);
}
```

We render the character whenever a key is pressed (keyPressed) directly on a black background using the font that we loaded in setup. Apart from setting the font and the textSize to be really large, we measure the text width by using textWidth and use this width to center the text on screen. Centering is a simple computation in which we take overall width of the canvas, subtract the text width from it, and then divide by two to get the space left of the character. We draw the character with this space between the left border of the canvas and the character as the x position. Done.

? Think about this

We explained the centering very quickly. Try to visualize the procedure on paper. Draw the canvas as a rectangle, the centered letter inside the canvas, and then the margins between the left and right border and the letter. If you measure the width of canvas, letter, and the margins, you can redo the preceding calculation.

Now that we have seen how to obtain characters and draw them centered on the canvas, we can take this to the next level by rendering the characters in indirect ways. The next example is a variation of the previous example. We render the letter by lots of tiny randomly placed dots. In the previous chapters, we have used randomness to place visual elements, but how can we place them randomly inside the character? We use a trick to do this: we draw the typed character on a separate canvas textCanvas in black and white whenever a key is pressed. Then we generate lots of dots randomly and check whether they are inside the character by comparing the random position of the dot to the color at the same position on the textCanvas. If the color is black, we have hit the space outside the character, and we don't draw the dot. If the color is white, then we hit the character, and we draw the dot on the original canvas. Let's see how this works.

Print the pressed key as a character within randomized dotting

```
PFont f;
PGraphics textCanvas;
void setup() {
  size(400, 400);
  textCanvas = createGraphics(400, 400);
  f = loadFont("InterUI-ExtraBold-250.vlw");
```

```
  background(0);
}
void draw() {}
void keyPressed() {
  // draw character on off-screen canvas
  textCanvas.beginDraw();
  textCanvas.textFont(f, 250);
  textCanvas.background(0);
  textCanvas.fill(255);
  textCanvas.textSize(250);
  // measure character width
  float charWidth = textCanvas.textWidth(key);
  // draw character centered
  textCanvas.text(key, (width-charWidth)/2, 300);
  textCanvas.endDraw();
  // draw new character
  background(0); noStroke();
  // go through 2000 iterations of the recursive
  // drawing of dots and thin lines
  for (int i = 0; i < 2000; i++) {
    drawDot(random(0, width), random(0, height), 10);
  }
}
void drawDot(float x, float y, int depth) {
  // stop recursion if depth is 0
  if (depth == 0) {
    return;
  }
  // look up the brightness of current position
  // in the textcanvas (where we drew the letter)
```

```
if (brightness(textCanvas.get((int)x, (int)y)) > 0) {
    // if inside letter, print a dot with some transparency
    // depending on the depth of recursion
    fill(255, map(depth, 0, 10, 80, 180));
    ellipse(x, y, depth/2, depth/2);
}
// find next position
float nextX = x + random(-20, 20);
float nextY = y + random(-20, 20);
// go into recursion on next level
drawDot(nextX, nextY, depth - 1);
}
```

Drawing the character on the separate canvas works exactly the same as for the normal Processing canvas (compare with the code in the previous example). When rendering to a separate canvas like this, don't forget to prepare and finalize the canvas with beginDraw() and endDraw(), respectively. This separate canvas is then used to look up whether a position on the canvas is inside the letter or outside. We do this by checking the brightness of the pixel at the precise position (using brightness(textCanvas.get((int)x, (int)y))) and comparing it to 0. Only if a position is inside a letter (i.e., brightness greater than 0), it will be rendered as a bright white dot on the visible Processing canvas. This results in a randomized "dotting" of the character. In other words, the character appears because there are only dots rendered within the bounds of the character. Try it out and note that this sketch needs a brief loading time before it is responsive.

? Think about this

Can you think how to achieve this example without recursion and a simple for loop? Not easy, but you are ready for this now. Try it out.

What is interesting in this example (Figure 4-7) is that we use a concept called recursion to go ten steps deep into a random position and draw dots according to whether the position is inside or outside the letter. Recursion means that we call the drawDot function from keyPressed, and then inside drawDot, we call the function itself again. This creates a loop as you can imagine. If we are not careful, this loop never ends and our sketch will crash quickly. We can avoid this and break out of the loop because every time we call drawDot, we decrease the last parameter depth. And at the beginning of drawDot, we check if depth is 0 and stop in this case. A simple return is enough to immediately "snap back" all the layers up to keyPressed.

We already play a bit with the transparency of the dots in the previous example (the deeper the recursion, the stronger the dot), but we can certainly go further. Let's add more decoration to the "dotted" character drawn: small transparent lines that give the character an almost organic feel. This is done with two small changes to the previous code.

___

Shortcut to change transparency of the dots from the previous code example

PREVIOUS:

```
// look up the brightness of current position
// in the text canvas (where we drew the letter)
if (brightness(textCanvas.get((int)x, (int)y)) > 100) {
    // if inside letter, print a solid dot
    fill(255, map(depth, 0, 10, 80, 180));
    ellipse(x, y, depth/2, depth/2);
```

NEW:

```
} else if (depth == 10) {
    // return if not found and this is the first level
    return;
```

```
}
// find next position
float nextX = x + random(-20, 20);
float nextY = y + random(-20, 20);
```

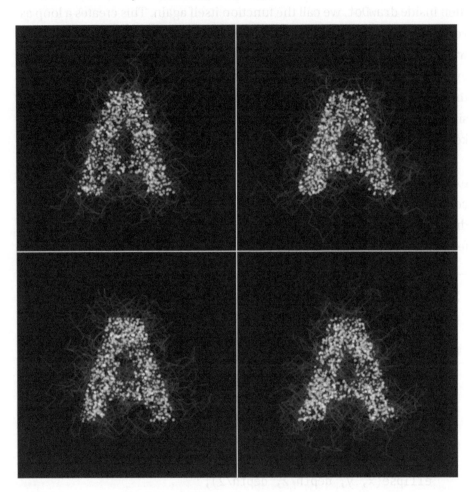

Figure 4-7. *Print the pressed key as a character within randomized dotting*

NEW:

```
// set the stroke color
stroke(180, map(depth, 0, 10, 20, 80));
// draw line from current to next point
line(x, y, nextX, nextY);

// go into recursion on next level
drawDot(nextX, nextY, depth - 1);
```

To draw transparent lines from the initially random positions in random directions, we just add a few lines before drawDot to set the stroke color and draw a line between the current and the next dot position. Even with just this change, the sketch will show interesting lines. However, the lines now also show up in the black space around the character (not good!). That's why we need to add a second change else if (depth == 10) to check whether a random position on the first level (where depth is 10) is outside a character and abort the recursion with return.

We have done it again: talk about an essential feature of Processing, keyboard input, and then mash it together with things we have seen before in book – randomness, drawing many things and functions. Also, we have introduced recursion in an easy way which is actually not the easiest computational concept. Well done, dear reader!

4.4.3 Other input

There are some other forms of input that can be used in Processing which include, but are not limited to, audio input from a microphone, full-body motion sensing from a Kinect device, hand and finger motion data from a Leap Motion device, and muscle contractions and arm movement data from a Myo band. And with some extra hardware, like an Arduino, you can sense a lot of interesting things: the brightness in your room, the moisture on your floor, the heartbeat of your partner, the speed of your motorcycle, and more. By using Processing libraries, it is also possible to design different interactions which gather input data even from multiple hardware devices.

You can use such input creatively and with similar mappings as what we did with the mouse and keyboard. For example, when you track a human skeleton with a Kinect camera or fingers of a human hand with a Leap Motion device, you will receive position data of fingers, joints, and centers of body parts. These positions are given either in 2D or 3D coordinates (x, y or x, y, z, respectively). It is not very difficult to collect these positions and map them to visual elements on the 2D canvas or in 3D space. A good starting point is to link different visual elements to the positions (hands, shoulders, hips, head) that you are interested in. This way, you will get a better feeling for how the input device measures your movements and where its limitations lie.

Here, you can make good use of the MemoryDot as well. By linking the input from devices or sensors to one or more MemoryDot objects, you can control its motion in a richer way than with mouse and keyboard. Play with the length of the memory and how you map the output to visual elements or influencing visual elements. You will soon understand which data are directly useful for your creative process and which data need more work.

The most common manual input devices used for designing interaction in Processing are the ones we introduced in more depth: keyboard and mouse. The mouse remains probably the most important control for creative work with Processing and to explore interactive, dynamic sketches. The keyboard input is helpful for triggering commands and switching between more than two states (for that, you have about 100 keys at your disposal). As we will see soon in the next chapter, mouse and keyboard are also very useful for testing and exploring new possibilities quickly.

4.5 Summary

So far, we have created more and more shapes, colors, randomness, and depth. It is time for the spotlight, for presenting our work to others. This is called the production phase, when we make things ready for printing or screening, where we make things stable to run for a longer time, and where we prepare the code for the next iterations. Why is the last thing so important? Nobody will actually see the code, right? Well, it's simple: when you go for the big stage or the opening event of your exhibition, you will need to make small adjustments quickly to match a new context, the exhibition space, the audience, or even just the broken projector in the venue. Having a clear code structure will help you in this stressful moment, when you really need everything to be right and beautiful. See it as a way to remove stress and remain calm when it matters.

There is also another reason: when you are in the moment of creation, the flow of getting immersed in your work with the machine, you know exactly where to find the code to change the color or to move an element less fast on the screen. This moment stops eventually, and you work on other projects for two or three weeks. The moment you return to messy code and a complex structure, you will feel lost, you will see code that does not seem to be yours anymore. Frustration is quite expected, until you go back into the moment of creation and refresh your mind.

It does not need to be so hard. Leave comments and traces for yourself, so your code and knowledge will snap together immediately. You will waste less time and get cracking fast.

Another benefit of clear structure is that you will be able to get help easier and faster. Any expert that you might find will be more willing to help you when they don't have to work with a mess and spend an hour to understand what you aimed for in the first place. We will come to this again in the last part where you will learn how to solve your problems step by step and how you get help fast.

Finally, and that is the main rationale in this chapter: creating depth and maintaining a structure that makes us comfortable to branch off in different, new directions. Only by iterating in this phase, lots and lots of times, we will be able to achieve depth in our work, depth that will be polished in the next chapter. Read on!

CHAPTER 5

Completion and production

In this last chapter of the first part, we show examples, tricks, and hints to help you reach the moment of completion. Creative work often aims at being shown, exposed, performed, perceived, reflected, and celebrated. All this happens not only at a creative level but also on the creation itself. The creative process spins extra fast in these moments, and getting work from "80%" to "100%" takes a lot of energy and perseverance (some people might refer to the "80/20" law here[1]). Although we would really like to present an easy recipe for success, there is none (that we know of). Instead, we will show you things that hopefully make your life easier toward completing your work for production. We start by getting your creative work to production resolution.

5.1 Making things big for print

This book is all about digital art and creation. So far, we have shown you how to create with code, playing with the almost unlimited possibilities of the digital realm. Yet, this is not always where you journey ends or is meant to end. Sometimes we have to physicalize our work for production, for instance, when preparing for print.

---

[1]The "80/20" principle is also called "Pareto principle."

© Yu Zhang, Mathias Funk 2021
Y. Zhang and M. Funk, *Coding Art*, https://doi.org/10.1007/978-1-4842-6264-1_5

When printing, rescaling, or rendering snapshots of your work, this section will show you ways of how to make your work big and solve potential problems.

If you have ever printed something in high quality, for instance, a really nice photo, you will have heard about DPI ("dots per inch"). DPI is a measure for how many printed dots fit into an inch and common values are 72, 150, 200, 300, and 600. For high-quality printing and viewing from a small distance, high DPI values are preferable.

Given a DPI value from your print shop, how to know the number of pixels you need? For this question, we also need to know how big your print will be. For example, if you want to print with 600 DPI on a 10cm by 10cm card, you will need to render a sketch of 2362 by 2362 pixels. This is far more than we have been rendering so far in this book. It's time to blow it up!

Before we go into that, let's use Processing to make these pixel calculations for us - it is work for a computer program after all:

Calculate pixels length from size and DPI values in Processing

```
// 100mm for 10cm
int sizeInMilliMeters = 100;
// 600 DPI
int desiredDPI = 600;
// output from Processing
print("Pixel length: ");
println(round((sizeInMilliMeters * desiredDPI)/25.4));
```

With this short program, Processing can calculate the pixel values for you; just fill in your specific printing size and DPI.

5.1.1 High-resolution rendering

How to render in a very high resolution? Printing needs high resolutions and perhaps even specific colors. We will show you here how to make your work large and save rendered images, so they can be printed or produced. Before you start, make a copy of the current version of your work. You will need this "small-scale" version of the sketch later on, for instance, to compare or to find the right moment to take a snapshot. In the previous examples, we have explained how to calculate the pixel size you would need when printing your work at a specific DPI resolution. Let's say, you want to render the following example sketch in the dimension 1000 by 1000 pixels:

Original canvas of 400 by 400 pixels

```
size(400, 400);
rect(40, 40, 200, 200);
```

The first thing that you might want to change (and you actually have to change) is the canvas `size`:

Change the canvas size to 1000 by 1000 pixels

```
size(1000, 1000);
rect(40, 40, 200, 200);
```

What happened? The canvas increased to 1000 by 1000 pixels, but the white square stayed at the same position and size as before. At this point, we have two different approaches that we can take: scaling the canvas or using size-dependent values. We don't recommend changing all values manually, because this is a lot of work for a larger sketch and you would have to do it all again, once you need a rendering in a different pixel size.

Scaling the canvas. The first approach is to leave the number as is and to introduce scale before rendering the rectangle:

Scale the drawing on the resized canvas

```
size(1000, 1000);
scale(1000/400.);
rect(40, 40, 200, 200);
```

What we did to determine the scale factor is to divide the new pixel amount (1000) by the previous pixel amount (400). By using 400. (with the extra dot) instead of 400, we can ensure that the division is a floating point division. That means the division can result in a more precise number. For example, we get 1000/400 = 2 with integer division and 1000/400. = 2.5 with floating point division. The latter is a better input for scale. You might have noticed this extra dot earlier in the book examples. The extra dot turns a number into a floating point number, which turns the entire division into a floating point division. We get a higher-precision output which is a good thing for scaling and rendering. The closer the numbers are that we divide (or the larger the number that we divide by), the more precision we need. Note that you need to insert scale before drawing anything, so at the beginning of the draw function.

Size-dependent values. The second approach is to make all values in the sketch depend on the size of the canvas. In our example, this would result in the following changes to the original code:

Use size-dependent values in code

```
size(400, 400);
rect(width/10., height/10., width/2., height/2.);
```

After this change, you can modify the canvas size as much as you like, and the location and size of the white rectangle will be proportionate.

Modify the canvas to achieve proportionately sized visuals

```
size(1000, 1000);
rect(width/10., height/10., width/2., height/2.);
```

Now some bad news: it is not easy to mix these two approaches in a single sketch. Mixing might lead to problems that are hard to identify and fix. Therefore, it is best to stick to one approach and make this also very clear in a comment at the beginning of the sketch.

If you try both approaches, did you notice something? Check the border of the white rectangle again. They are thicker in the scaling example. The reason is that scaling influences all drawing operations, not just positioning and sizing. It influences in the same way border thickness (stroke weight) and other scalable properties of visual elements. So, if you use the scaling approach, make sure that you check and adjust the stroke weight and other visual properties before rendering overnight.

5.1.2 Migrating to scalable version

The preceding approaches are quite straightforward when starting out with a new creative work. What do we do if our work is there already in a complex sketch, and we need to scale it? You can pick any example from this book and follow a simple process depending on which approach you choose.

Scaling approach. Use the Processing "search and replace" function and replace "width" and "height" with their values as used in size. Add scale at the beginning of setup and draw (and also if you are drawing in a different function). Test and save this copy.

Size-dependent values. Go through the entire code and replace any value that is relevant for scaling (position, size, stroke weight, etc.) with an expression depending on width or height. We have done this in the earlier example which is copied here again.

Use values in code depending on width or height

```
size(1000, 1000);
// all values are now depending on width or height
rect(width/10., height/10., width/2., height/2.);
```

Still not sure how to choose for an approach? Ok, here is a rule of thumb: if your code uses few transformations like translate, rotate, and scale, then the scaling approach is the right choice. If you use a lot of transformations, changing the values might be a lot of work, but ultimately less trouble than figuring out transformation problems. Finally, this decision also depends on how well your code is organized and how cleanly you have separated transformations with pushMatrix and popMatrix. This is also the reason why we suggested making copies of your code before: you can always try one approach and move the other approach if that seems to work out better. Even better, consider using a version control system such as "git" which allows you to track fine-grained changes in your code.

Reminder   Search online for "git version control system". You will find a lot of technical information, but there are also very easy graphical clients for git available. You might want to visit the sites of popular git-hosting companies such as https://github.com or https://gitlab.com.

When you run your code at a high resolution, please be aware that it might take longer to render and that the frame rate will go down, especially sketches with a lot of rendering operations or loops with many iterations will have this problem. Interaction with the mouse will be more difficult and sometimes become useless, because rendering a single large frame takes several to complete. For these problems, read on, there are ways to solve them.

5.1.3 Rendering snapshots of dynamic work

We have seen how we can get our work to the right resolution (pixel size). High resolutions might take far longer to render than our "working" sketches. That's ok, because we let the sketches render and then take printable snapshots at the right moment.

What does it mean to "take a snapshot" in Processing? It means that Processing briefly stops the draw loop and saves the current canvas to a file. You can customize the name and type of image file and even ask Processing to count up in the file name, so the order of snapshots is preserved (image-0001.png, image-0002.png, image-0003.png, etc.). The following code shows how this works:

Take a snapshot in Processing with saveFrame

```
void setup() {
    size(400, 400);
}
void draw() {
    background(0);
    for(int i = 0; i < 20; i++) {
        ellipse(random(0, 400), random(0, 400), 20, 20);
        // save the canvas as a PNG image file, include
        // a four-digit enumeration in the file name
        saveFrame("image-####.png");
    }
```

155

The saveFrame renders the canvas in the state when saveFrame is called, so putting it at the end of the draw function is a good choice. Before you can save frames, make sure that you have saved the sketch in a local folder where you can find it. All saved frames will go to this folder. Now, if you run this code, and wait for a while, you will see lots and lots of image files appearing in the sketch folder. Processing can save images in several formats, basically files ending in ".tif", ".jpg", or ".png" (according to the Processing reference). In short, ".tif" files are often uncompressed and quite big, and ".jpg" files use lossy compression, which means smaller files and lower quality (not ideal for printing). Finally, ".png" files use compression without reducing quality (our choice in all examples). You can find more information about these different formats on the Internet. Back to rendering files in Processing: if the file name includes hash marks ("#"), they will be replaced by the current value of frameCount when calling saveFrame. The result is a series of numbered images that show every single rendered frame. We can use this to pick the best frames (this is what we did for illustrating this book), or you can make an animated GIF to share on social media (if that's your thing).

Unless we want a whole series of rendered frames, rendering and saving all frames is not exactly our goal. With this function, we can render any frame that we would like, so why not be more selective? Our next example shows how to trigger saving a single frame with a key press:

Save a single frame in Processing with a key press

```
void setup() {
    size(400, 400);
}
void draw() {
    background(0);
```

```
  for(int i = 0; i < 20; i++) {
    ellipse(random(0, width), random(0, height), 20, 20);
  }
}
void keyPressed() {
  // save the canvas as a PNG image file, include
  // a four-digit enumeration in the file name
  saveFrame("image-####.png");
}
```

This is almost exactly the same code with the only change that we moved the frame saving part to the new keyPressed function. This sketch will not save every single frame, but instead wait for a key press (any key should work!) and only then save the current frame. This allows us to watch the frames go by and hit the keyboard to save the ones we like.

Tips   Frames change too fast? Use frameRate() in setup to adjust the frame rate. Try values of 2, 1, 0.5 or even 0.3.

This approach to selecting a frame works for sketches that still render in a reasonable time (less than a few seconds per frame). If we go really big, then a frame might take tens of seconds or longer to render. Unless we don't mind a really long wait for the right moment, there is another approach: selecting the frame by its number.

We work in two steps. First, go back to the original (not scaled) copy of your sketch. In this original sketch, you need to insert the following function at the end.

Reminder   Remember that we suggested that you make a copy
before scaling stuff? Always make copies of your work, especially
when you plan to make a bigger change.

Print out the `frameCount` on the Processing console

```
void keyPressed() {
    // print out the current frame number
    println(frameCount);
}
```

This handler for key presses will simply print out the `frameCount` on
the Processing console. We can now run the original sketch and hit a key
when we see an interesting frame that we would like to render big later on.
The printed `frameCount` values are printed on the console and need to be
copied into a text editor or noted down for the second step. Run the sketch
as long as you like and collect the frame numbers.

In the second step, we insert a short code snippet in the scaled version
of our sketch, at the end of the `draw` function. Let's say, we have done the
first step and hit the keyboard for an interesting frame, which printed
`frameCount` 108 on the console. Now we can use this number to render
and save exactly this frame in the scaled version of the sketch.

Print out `frameCount` number to render and save the exact frame we want

```
void draw() {
    // draw code from sketch
    // ...
```

NEW:

```
    if(frameCount == 108) {
      saveFrame("image-####.png");

      // optional: quit sketch after rendering
      System.exit(0);
    }
}
```

When we run this code, the sketch will check the current `frameCount` after drawing the frame contents, and if it equals "our" frame number 108, Processing will save the canvas to an image file "image-0108.png". Now we should be ready to run this sketch in a long, very long rendering operation – possibly through the night – and receive a beautiful, large-scale rendered frame for breakfast. The optional extra line `System.exit(0)` will stop the running sketch after saving the frame. Might be helpful if you are rendering overnight, so your computer can go to sleep mode and you save the earth (a little bit).

This should be a working recipe for sketches that do not require user input. However, we have made avid use of the mouse in this book, so you might have created a sketch that uses mouse input to generate its most beautiful (or most interesting) frames. How to render these when you are sleeping? Let's go back to what we said earlier in the previous chapter. Any kind of interaction and user input is data. Such data can be recorded and also simulated if necessary. That means we don't need real-time input if we want to reproduce an interactive sketch. Imagine the following simple example:

Original code example of ellipse following the mouse position

```
void setup() {
    size(400, 400);
}
```

```
void draw() {
    background(0);
    for(int i = 0; i < 20; i++) {
      ellipse(random(0, mouseX), random(0, height), 5, 5);
    }
}
```

This sketch renders 20 random dots per frame, but only left of the mouse position. Clearly, this sketch is highly dependent on the mouse input. How to reproduce a frame with a particular mouse position?

The first step is again to obtain the precise position. We add a simple function to the sketch to record the current mouse position when we click the mouse.

Print out the current mouse position when clicking the mouse

```
void mouseClicked() {
    // print out the current mouse position
    println(mouseX, mouseY);
}
```

Similar to how we record the frameCount by pressing a key on the keyboard, a mouse click will record x and y position of the mouse. We can take this data and extend the sketch with the following line. For example, our desired horizontal mouse position is recorded as 180 on the Processing console. The following code will render the sketch with that mouse position (unless we move the mouse over the sketch window):

Render the sketch with predefined mouse position

```
void setup() {
    size(400, 400);
```

```
NEW:
    mouseX = 180;
}
void draw() {
    background(0);
    for(int i = 0; i < 20; i++) {
      ellipse(random(0, mouseX), random(0, height), 5, 5);
    }
}
```

This works for the mouse position, but also other interactive input can be scripted or turned into variables that can then be scripted. We will talk about similar issues in the next section: "backstaging" a sketch with some sort of remote control.

5.2 A backstage for control

It is important that we can easily control different settings of our Processing sketches or that we can easily change values in various places when testing, presenting, and exhibiting our work in different contexts. Here we explain three useful tools for that: (1) using Processing's Tweak mode, (2) centralizing control with variables, and (3) using keyboard as a backstage.

From the first chapter on, we suggested that you prototype directly in code and try out new ideas and then immediately run the code. This helps you get into the Processing environment and train your code writing and reading skills (also called "code literacy"). It will also make you more fluent in generally expressing your ideas through coding. We hope you have made some big steps so far!

When it comes to fine-tuning your creative work, this often means changing values in various places in the code – not so much working with the general structure or reshaping visual elements.

5.2.1 Tweak mode in Processing

The creators of Processing have probably found this a problem as well, and they introduced the "Tweak" mode in Processing from version 3. Tweak mode adds a layer of sliders and color selectors on top of the source code of your sketch and allows to change most values while the sketch is running. Sounds like magic! To give you a better idea, try the following code:

Code example for testing Processing's Tweak mode

```
void setup() {
    size(400, 400);
    colorMode(HSB);
}
void draw() {
    background(0);
    fill(80, 120, 150);
    stroke(120, 255, 150);
    strokeWeight(12);
    ellipse(50, 200, 50, 50);
}
```

Before you can use the Tweak mode, you need to save this sketch on your computer. After that, you can select "Tweak" from the "Sketch" menu and run the sketch in Tweak mode. At first sight, everything seems normal, but then you will see small sliders on top of your source code. Move your mouse over one of these sliders and drag it left or right. Observe the changes in your running sketch. For example, try to center the circle on the canvas and to change its colors to a bright yellow or orange. With Processing's Tweak mode, this should be done in a matter of seconds.

? Think about this

Interesting question here: is this also coding? We think it is, because the Tweak mode lets you program in a highly interactive way.

After you stop a sketch running in Tweak mode, Processing will ask you whether you would like to keep the changes that you made using the sliders and color controls. If you confirm, the new values will be copied into your code for later use. Processing's Tweak mode works on variables, too. Let's see what you can do with variables in the next part.

5.2.2 Centralizing control with variables

When changing small things in your code, you sometimes notice that for testing a specific effect or look or behavior, you always need to change several values at the same time. For example, to test how a certain color would look like on a shape in the context of other visual elements. We often have to adjust these other elements as well. Check this example:

Code example for testing a specific effect (continued as follows)

```
void setup() {
    size(400, 400); noStroke();
}
void draw() {
    colorMode(HSB);
    background(175, 255, 10);
    fill(175, 155, 255);
```

```
  rect(200, 20, 100, 100);
  for(int i = 0; i < 20; i++) {
    fill(random(175, 200), 255, 255, 50);
    ellipse(random(0, mouseX), random(0, height), 50, 50);
  }
  fill(175, 255, 155);
  rect(20, 200, 100, 100);
}
```

Imagine that you look out of the window in your room right now. You see trees and wonder whether the earlier example sketch would perhaps look better in green. If you would want to make this change quickly, you would need to change a color value (because we are HSB mode, it would be the hue directly) in four different places. As it happens, you might forget one and have to go back after spotting the mistake. This is avoidable with a single variable mainColor that drives all color statements.

Use a single variable mainColor that drives all color statements

```
void draw() {
  colorMode(HSB);
  // 175 for blue, 100 for green in HSB mode
  int mainColor = 175;
  background(mainColor, 255, 10);
  fill(mainColor, 155, 255);
  rect(200, 20, 100, 100);
  for(int i = 0; i < 20; i++) {
    fill(random(mainColor, mainColor + 25), 255, 255, 50);
    ellipse(random(0, mouseX), random(0, height), 50, 50);
  }
}
```

```
    fill(mainColor, 255, 155);
    rect(20, 200, 100, 100);
}
```

As we can see in the preceding changed code, we replace the concrete value 175 by the variable `mainColor` in four lines. In three cases, this is a simple replacement. In the line where the color is used in the `random` call, we have to add an expression `mainColor + 25` to replace 200 as well. Now all colors in this sketch follow the `mainColor` and can be adjusted with a single change at the top of the `draw` function. Try this also in Tweak mode.

5.2.3 "Backstaging" with the keyboard

We have seen that we can link values in our code to sliders and control using the Tweak mode. This mode is great for exploring and experimenting with visual elements. Perhaps, we also need some control during showtime, as we want to switch to different scenarios or quickly reset the sketch without having to restart the program.

Let's try the first one: how to switch between different visuals just using the keyboard?

Use the keyboard to switch between different visuals

```
void setup() {
    size(400, 400);
    noStroke(); colorMode(HSB);
    rectMode(CENTER);
}
void draw() {
    background(0);
```

```
if(key == '1') {
  fill(50, 155, 255);
  rect(width/2, height/2, 100, 100);
}
else if(key == '2') {
  fill(100, 155, 255);
  ellipse(width/2, height/2, 100, 100);
}
else if(key == '3') {
  fill(150, 155, 255);
  rect(width/2, height/2, 100, 100);
}
else if(key == '4') {
  fill(200, 155, 255);
  ellipse(width/2, height/2, 100, 100);
} else {
  fill(0, 0, 50);
  ellipse(width/2, height/2, 100, 100);
}
}
```

This example shows a very simple approach for switching between five states: four colorful shapes for keys "1", "2", "3", and "4" and a single default shape for any other key pressed. We don't use a keyboard handler such as keyPressed. Instead, we simply compare the key variable to different characters on the keyboard. The final else part ensures that we show a default shape in case all comparisons fail (because you may have pressed the letter "s") or no key is pressed at the moment. You can use any character your keyboard provides, but be especially careful with letters of the alphabet ("a", "b", "c", etc.) because they exist in two versions: uppercase and lowercase. You would not imagine how many panicking students came to us minutes before an important demo just because their CAPS LOCK key had been pressed accidentally. Funny, right? Not in their situation.

? Think about this

Try changing the size of the rectangle at a key press. Using a variable, It Is not so difficult; see earlier.

In this example (Figure 5-1), we use the keyboard to switch between shapes and colors. This is only a simple example. You can use the keyboard to switch between different functions controlling many things or create a switchable demo of all examples in this book. As a final example for "backstaging," let's make a sketch that uses the keyboard to reset.

Use the keyboard to reset the visual output

```
void setup() {
    size(400, 400);
    background(0); noStroke(); rectMode(CENTER);
}
void draw() {
    fill(40 + 20 * noise(0.8 - frameCount/2000.), 155,
    noise(frameCount/100.) * 255, random(10, 200));
    rect(width * noise(0.2 + frameCount/100.), height *
    noise(0.3 + frameCount/200.), 100, 100);
}
void keyPressed(){
    background(0);
}
```

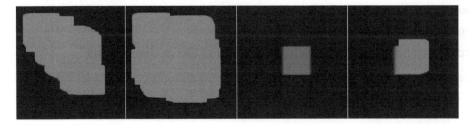

Figure 5-1. *Example of how we can reset the canvas after drawing frame over frame*

? Think about this

Try saving a specific frame of this sketch. If you save the same frame multiple times, do they look different? Why?

This sketch uses lots of randomness to generate a green-blue rectangle painting erratically on a black canvas. We can use the keyboard handler keyPressed to redraw the background and thereby clear the canvas.

In this section, we have seen how we can use some sort of backstaging techniques to control different aspects of our Processing sketches. We can use the Tweak mode in Processing to adjust values directly. We use variables as centralized control points to change values all over the Processing sketch, and we use the keyboard to switch and change the behavior of running sketches. We did not touch upon creating graphical user interface (GUI) elements for control on top of our sketch, which is possible with a Processing GUI library like ControlP5.[2] And now, let's make this all better by looking at how to improve stability and reliability of our code.

---

[2]The ControlP5 library is directly available from the Processing library manager. It is worth looking at its project website and reading the documentation. If you need user interface elements in your sketch, this library is probably the easiest way to go. Make sure that you use the newest version and keep this in mind when you search for help online.

5.3 More stable and less risky code

We stay with the real-time aspects of creating and running Processing code in this section and give you a few pointers to make your code more stable and reliable under difficult production conditions (that differ from your own setup). While we will not solve or prescribe how to solve every problem that might occur in your journey, we will give you hints what you can do better.

5.3.1 The right things in the right place

Have you seen hiccups, delays in rendering, or that Processing slows down more and more and eventually crashes? All of these symptoms point to things being done at the wrong time (or in the wrong code location). Just take the following code:

Test the speed of running a Processing's sketch

```
void setup() {
    size(1000, 1000);
}
void draw() {
    PGraphics texture = createGraphics(1000, 1000);
    texture.beginDraw();
    texture.background(0);
    // draw more things here...
    texture.endDraw();
    tint(255, 20);
    image(texture, 0, 0);
}
```

Does anything strike your attention here? Although this sketch should run at an ok speed in your computer, it runs far slower than it should. How do we know? Well, we can just print the frame rate on the Processing console to check.

Print out the frame rate on the Processing console

```
void draw() {
    // all other code as before

NEW:
    println(frameRate);
}
```

By adding the last line in the draw function, we get a running output of the current frame rate. Keep in mind that this sketch should run at 60 frames per second (fps). It could be easily half that frame rate on your computer. Why is that? If you look closer, you will find the first line of the draw function interesting. This line creates space in memory for a new texture of 1 million pixels (1000 times 1000). That sounds like a lot of work. Let's move this line from draw to setup and see how the frame rate changes.

Speed up a Processing's sketch rate by rearranging the code

```
PGraphics texture;
void setup() {
  size(1000, 1000);
  texture = createGraphics(1000, 1000);
}
void draw() {
  texture.beginDraw();
  texture.background(0);
```

170

```
// draw more things here...
texture.endDraw();
tint(255, 20);
image(texture, 0, 0);
println(frameRate);
}
```

This changed sketch runs quite a bit faster as you can see from the frame rate. Apparently, just changing the code location of createGraphics makes a big difference. It is not all good yet, because the frame rate is still less than 60fps, but it is a step. If you would peek in the TaskManager (on Windows) or Activity Monitor (on macOS), you would see a huge difference between the memory consumption of the first and the second version.

How can we generalize this into a rule of thumb? Any Processing command starting with "create…" or "load…" should be considered a bit more intensive because they are about reserving memory or loading resources like images, fonts, or audio files from hard disk. Even in the age of very fast hard disks (SSDs), this is quite slow compared to everything else happening in Processing. So: Move these calls and anything that you do only once to prepare drawing to setup. Don't run this kind of code in draw or, worse, in a for loop in draw. Again, anything that takes more time; only do it once (not 20, 60, or 1000 times). And double-check by looking at the frame rate (and memory consumption)!

Coming to another related source of potential problems. Did you notice that the change from the first to the second version with createGraphics in setup implies that we create a global variable for texture? What we did is we change the local variable texture in the first version to become a global variable texture in the second version.

Wait a minute, what are global and local variables anyway? This is a question of variable scope, that is, for which part of the code the variable is "visible." Global variables are globally (= entire program) visible. That means they are always available and can be accessed in every single line of the program. This sounds good at first, but an accessible variable can also be changed at every single line of the code. You can imagine how complex this can get if you are not careful. Next to global variables, there are local variables. As you can guess, local variables are not globally accessible. They have their own scope, a part of the code that they are defined and used in. Usually, we don't need to be too careful with local variables in functions or for loops. They are not visible outside their scope and therefore cannot cause harm. However, and that is the problem here, what happens if you give a local variable the same name as a global variable? The local variable claims the spot and takes over. When we want to change the global variable, only the local variable receives the change and the global one stays unchanged. This kind of problem happens often when we make changes to code, when we move variables from local to global and accidentally leave the local variable in place. Processing will probably not complain about this, but the results will be strange. So, repeating our earlier message about very carefully modifying the code structure: do this step by step and check afterward that all old artifacts are gone. This is another form of restructuring that we have seen earlier in the book. Handle with care.

5.3.2 Avoiding resource bloat

Even if you do things by the book (this book!) in terms of loading files at the right moment, Processing might still crash and return you a cryptic warning about memory. Sometimes content can be too big to fully load or to render smoothly. This is especially important for media files such as audio, videos, animated GIFs, and large image files. When Processing loads these files, it will often decompress them in memory (for faster access and rendering support). That means the file size on your hard disk might not be the final size in memory. Whenever you see Processing crash or abort while loading files, it is good to check their size and to try loading smaller files or fewer of them. This way you can spot the problematic file and then think of ways to fix it or design around it. For example, image files come in various resolutions, file formats, and compression variants. Try experimenting with different resolution or image format. Perhaps you don't need full 24 bit color depth because your sketch will draw the image with a `tint` anyway? There is usually a solution (see also the last part of the book).

5.3.3 Code structure

The question "is my code structured well?" is hard to answer in general. Instead, we would like you to develop your own capabilities to judge this in the context of your creative work. Understandability is often mentioned as an important criterion of code quality; however, this is difficult to assess in the moment of writing the code or just after. The true test comes after a few weeks or months, when you read your code again and the concepts are not that present in your mind anymore. At this moment, you will see whether your code is understandable to yourself (still easier than to others).

A first hint toward writing good code is to use meaningfully named variables and functions in all sketches. Things like `'int a, b, c; float f;'` should not happen. Yes, you planned to name everything properly later on. Got it, but no! This moment "later on" usually never happens, because the more code you write and the more you use the variables, the more the required efforts grow to fix them.[3] Therefore, make choosing good names a habit. There are only a few cases where very short variables are commonly accepted, for instance, as counters `i, j, k` in `for` loops or array indexes in complex algorithms. And `x, y, z` for space coordinates is fine, too.

Other ways to look at code quality are about the length of functions and their complexity. Researchers have investigated whether long and complex functions negatively affect understanding, and – surprise! – they do. As a rule of thumb, try to split functions up if they cover more than half a screen page, or even ten lines. Still, give them a meaningful name. What about complexity? Mostly this refers to control structures like `if ... else` and loops such as `for`. The more they occur in a single function and the more levels they have, the harder it is for human readers to fully understand the control flow in the function. Again, the recommendation is to split things up into properly named functions that do one thing right and not five to six things somehow mixed up. There is also another view of how to divide functions: think about the smallest meaningful task that a function could perform in your work. That's a good size for a function, and this ensures that you know exactly what this function does and how you can build onto it.

When you look the entire Processing sketch, use the same principles of splitting up into functions, when moving code to additional tabs in Processing. Creating a new tab is very simple, and you can cut/paste the code there and continue working. Give the tab a recognizable name, for instance, name according to functionality: "input_functions," "data_processing," or "rendering_output." Alternatively, name them according to

---

[3]This is called technical debt, which basically means that every time we make an easy decision, for example, to not comment or to leave something a little broken or unfinished, we incur some sort of debt that we will have to pay back at a later point. And everyone knows how debt works: it gets worse and worse.

different components: if you use classes like "Particle" or "MemoryDot," each should get its own tab. Then it will be easier to find your code back at a later moment.

Reminder   By the way, whenever you ask for help, use "Auto Format" before. Otherwise, it's just rude to the person you are asking for help. Their job is already hard enough: reading someone else's code is not easy (especially without comments).

Code structure is also a visual structure. If you look closely at all code examples in this book, you see that we use a visual structure in the code examples that is very consistent. We indent lines in functions, if ... else structures, for loops, and classes. This allows us to quickly scan the code. Reading well-formatted code is much easier for us because our brains can make sense of the shapes and structure long before reading the characters. The best thing is that this code format comes for free in Processing. Just select "Auto Format" from the "Edit" menu or press Ctrl+T (Cmd+T on macOS). This is the programming equivalent to zero-calorie comfort food, really.

Our last hint might be a bit controversial (if you talk to programmers): don't use classes to combine functions unless there is data that needs encapsulation as well. Treat classes (e.g., class Particle) as containers for data and data-specific functions. It might be tempting to structure your code with classes (especially if you have learned about classes in a programming course), but resist this temptation; your creative process can move faster and freer without a rigid structure that you planned out carefully. If at all, structure will grow with your work as you need it. Especially when thinking about class hierarchies ("class cat is part of class feline, class feline is part of class animal, class lion is part of class feline, etc."), stop there. Think of something beautiful and use a Processing tab instead. Almost anything can be better done with additional Processing tabs and properly named functions. Quality code is not about showing how smart you are.

5.3.4 Don't reinvent the wheel

Many times, we might need to crack a problem in Processing that feels difficult to us at first. For example, moving a line tangentially along a curve, which would require even a trained programmer some time to figure out (including reading about geometry and trigonometric functions, trying out a first implementation, getting it right in all cases, making it fast and reliable, etc.). Save yourself the trouble. Most problems that you might experience have occurred to others before, and many of them are even covered in the Processing library. Ok, let's try "moving a line tangentially along a curve." We are pretty sure that this has been done before. If we search in the Processing reference for curve and tangent (a straight line that touches a curve at a point), then we find several interesting functions: curve, curvePoint, and curveTangent. The Processing reference even shows us how to use them. We just need to play a bit with the values for drawing the curve and then change how the tangent is used. Also, the example is looped by using frameCount with modulo (%) operator (Figure 5-2).

Figure 5-2. *Example of animating a line parallel to a curve point in a loop*

Create a loop in Processing by using `frameCount` with modulo (%) operator

```
void setup() {
  size(400, 400); noFill();
}
```

```
void draw() {
  background(0); stroke(255, 0, 0);
  // draw the curve from point 100, 100 to 300, 300
  // the first and last two parameters are control points
  // that give the curve some 'curve'
  curve(200, -400, 100, 100, 300, 300, 200, 800);
  float t = (frameCount % 200) / 200.;
  float x = curvePoint(200, 100, 300, 200, t);
  float y = curvePoint(-400, 100, 300, 800, t);
  float tx = curveTangent(200, 100, 300, 200, t) / 5.;
  float ty = curveTangent(-400, 100, 300, 800, t) / 5.;
  // set line color depending on the angle (tx/ty)
  stroke(atan2(tx, ty) * 255, 0, 255);
  // draw our line
  line(x - tx, y - ty, x + tx, y + ty);
}
```

? Think about this

What is the lesson here? If you meet a challenge in Processing that seems overwhelmingly hard or at least difficult, and you think you might need some hours to get it sorted out, then think again.

Describe the problem in clear terms and search for them, either in the Processing reference or in a search engine online. Follow the leads, check what people have tried, and change your search terms toward more accurate ones. In the preceding example, the challenge might have been to identify the key term "tangent" if we were just thinking of "a line moving next to a curve." Still, searching for "curve" will get us to curve in the Processing reference, from which curveTangent is linked or can be found close by.

Tips   When you think and describe your problem in new words, and then again, your mind will form new connections, which might even lead to the solution directly. Even if you cannot find the solution by yourself, you will have learned something valuable.

What are the benefits of using code from Processing directly or from a library? First of all, you save time, you don't need to "reinvent the wheel." You often get a better function that covers more cases and is more robust than what you would implement. And we don't mean that you could not do it. We mean that you are trying to solve a very specific problem that might bring you to a very specific implementation of the function, which might not work anymore once your specific problem evolves to something else (it usually does!). Therefore, it is good to rely on a more general implementation of this functionality. Most likely this function has been built by someone who knows how to do it, and it has been reviewed and tested by others. Having more people involved makes a big difference in quality: they all have different problems which the function needs to match, so chances are that the function is quite stable and reliable by now. Finally, by looking at how others approached the problem with the function will teach you something about Processing, about terminology, and about the interface that the function represents. Processing functions and their structure follow a certain philosophy, and getting to know this way of thinking will help you indirectly with future problems.

5.4 Testing before deployment

Producing your work outside of your home and studio setup means preparing your work in advance for a somewhat unknown context. Your code might be run on a different computer, using a different screen or projector. In your planning, please reserve some time for this. Do not run the creative phase till the day of the big event. Stop the creative phase in time, to prepare for development. It is a matter of respect for your audience and for your own creative work. In this section, we will focus on testing and preparation for such a deployment.

5.4.1 Depending on dependencies

The first thing to be aware of is that Processing is one of your dependencies for deployment. What is a dependency really? It is a condition for your work to run, to be performed, or to be produced for an audience. Without this dependency, it will not work. In the case of Processing sketches, Processing itself is a dependency. You need to ensure that the computer available in the venue can run Processing, and not just that: it needs to be the same (or a later) version of Processing and also running with similar hardware (processor speed and memory, graphics card, and sound equipment) and software like the operating system. The more similar the venue's system is to your own, the better the transition will work.

If you are using Processing libraries to achieve a part of the functionality, these libraries are also dependencies. Without the libraries, your code will not work or produce inferior output. Finally, your sketch might be broken into multiple tabs and resource files (usually in the "data" folder of the sketch folder). Make sure that all these files are transferred to the venue's system by copying the entire sketch folder.

Processing actually supports in this transition by allowing to "export [an] application" (available from the "File" menu). This tool will create a self-contained bundle of all parts necessary to run your sketch. Self-contained means that all parts are packaged and no dependencies are lost. This is great to "freeze" your project in a state ready for showtime. Try that, but keep in mind that this "frozen" state does not allow you to tweak things in the venue anymore (but just in case, see next section). For that, always keep a source version with you.

5.4.2 Anticipating differences

The transition to a production context means anticipating potential problems beforehand: Your guest account has expired. The Internet may be slow. Your power supply may not work. The computer has no VGA video output anymore. No HDMI video output (yet). Windows decides to install new updates. Your battery is dead. The beamer's RED color channel does not show. There are no loudspeakers available. And more. This is hard. Only experience (making lots of mistakes) will allow you to do this really well. And still problems will happen. Our advice is to overthink it, but not to worry. Brainstorm about what might go wrong when moving to a different computer or even a different system setup. Would a different screen be trouble? Think about not just different resolutions but also about aspect ratio ("sorry, we only have a square projection area ...") or lighting conditions ("directly next to the window").

We can prepare for these challenges, for instance, by using "backstaging" (see beginning of this chapter) to prepare for deployment. We can make changes for aspect ratio and screen resolution quick to solve by introducing scaling and variables (also for adjusting the color to a projection surface). We can even add interactive controls to our work, so we can quickly intervene if something goes wrong during setup or the performance.

When traveling with a computer and aiming to present work somewhere else, there are general hints. Bring sufficiently many USB sticks with a backup of your work. Also, bring your own laptop including charger and power socket adapters. Don't forget spare cables and connectors, for instance, for connecting and converting HDMI and VGA (for visual output) or different plugs and cables for audio output including audio interfaces and amplifiers.

And yet, all tricks of trade come short to planning and communicating ahead. Communicate clearly with the other side what the expectations are and be aware that details matter. Ask about the room and the technical setup. Visit the space in person, if possible, and check it out for yourself.

Work it out like famous rock stars (well, their production crew) and write a rider. This is a document that details your physical setup on a stage or other venue, your equipment needs, and what kinds of (human) support or expertise you need to have available on site. Again, it will help if you brainstorm what might go wrong or what crazy mistakes could happen (so they don't, with a bit of luck and good preparation). Finally, think about using similar equipment or a similar location as in the exhibition space to prepare. Every step that you take and every problem that you solve before moving to the exhibition space allow you to spend more time adjusting your work to the venue and fine-tuning the experience.

5.4.3 Preparing for unattended operation

When deploying your work in an exhibition setting, it might be installed there for some time (days, weeks, or even months). There is a chance that you will not be there 24/7 and operate your work. Instead, there are people who are volunteering or employed by the venue to maintain an installation. The best you can do is making it extremely easy for these people to restart or repair your installation in case something goes wrong. In the end, visitors who encounter a broken installation will in some way attribute it negatively to you, the creative, not the support people.

What also looks broken is a screen saver that switches on after one hour and shows "Bob's computer" in a rotating font or, worse, a slide show of your personal photos from last summer. To avoid these kinds of slightly embarrassing events, switch off energy saving, a screen saver, Wi-Fi (if network access is not needed in your work), and a virus scanner. Move the computer (including mouse and keyboard, unless needed) out of the reach of visitors and secure it. You can test this before quite easily.

It helps when you prepare your work in such a way that it can be started and restarted within minutes and needs very few interactions to activate. Also think about how the installation needs to be shut down at the end of the day. What can be damaged if someone pulls the plug? Don't think nobody will do that, eventually; there are always cleaners, security people, fire inspectors, and the occasional curious visitor (or their 6-year-old child). The second point is about writing a clear manual for how to restart the installation, such as "start computer, wait for ..., double-click the ..., wait for ..., check that ... is visible, then move mouse pointer out of the screen." Provide contact details, so people can reach you in case nothing works. Hopefully, your phone stays silent and social media explodes (with positive reactions).

5.5 Moving to mobile

When we say "mobile," we mean "on the Web" – in a form that mobile devices can access it. There are other ways to address mobile users, for instance, with an app. However, developing apps is really beyond this book. There is an Android plugin for Processing that might work for you, give it a try.

Back to "mobile" and "on the Web." We include this part in the chapter not to introduce a whole new platform. Instead, the point is broadening your perspective on what it means to bring your work to different screens aligned with a diverse audience. Even installations in a location like a gallery, museum, or art center can benefit from shifting your work to the mobile Web, because it can be presented using tablets flat on the walls, instead of screens connected to computers connected to peripherals connected to a power socket. A tablet can present your work in different ways than a computer, because it allows for (multi-)touch input and a very high resolution. Tablets are available in many venues already. Another way to present your work is to ask local and remote visitors to open it on their personal smart phones or tablets. Exhibitions often provide QR codes that can be scanned with a smart phone camera, and the work opens in the mobile browser instantly.

In this section, we first explain the general structure of mobile Processing content, then dive into making the switch between Processing and p5.js, and finally explain more about the infrastructure necessary for hosting this content online.

5.5.1 Structure of mobile Processing content

When you run a sketch in Processing, Processing will provide your sketch with a runtime environment that gives your sketch access to all functionality of Processing and its libraries, the file system (e.g., the "data" folder), and also computer resources like a screen and audio equipment. When producing a Processing sketch for the (mobile) Web, all this is provided in some way by the local web browser of the visitor (or a tablet hanging on the wall of a gallery). That means your sketch needs to be modified such that it can run in a variety of web browsers (different people have different computers, right?). Also, these browsers have their own language and formats that need to be matched.

The simplest way of moving your work to the Web is by embedding it in a web page. A web page is written in HTML, a markup language that is based on tags like "<html>", "<div>", and "<a href="codingart.com">". Inside the HTML structure, we can often find two other languages, one for styling which is called CSS (search online for more information) and JavaScript, which we will use in the following. Remember that we explained that Processing works with the Java language behind the scenes? P5.js, the web version of Processing, works with JavaScript in the background. As the name suggests, the two languages Java and JavaScript are quite similar. Let's get started with a simple web page.

A template for rendering p5.js code in a web browser

```html
<html>
  <head>
    <script src="https://cdnjs.cloudflare.com/ajax/libs/p5.js
        /0.9.0/p5.js"></script>
    <script type="text/javascript">

        // this is a comment in Javascript
        //
        // insert p5.js code below
        //

        function setup() {
            // setup code
        }
        function draw() {
            // draw loop
        }
    </script>
  </head>
  <body></body>
</html>
```

The preceding code will be our template for the next examples. This code is the bare minimum that you need to render p5.js code in a web browser. You enter this code in a text editor (not Processing!). You can use either the built-in text editor of your operating system, or download an editor like Sublime Text, Atom, or Visual Studio Code.

After entering the preceding code, save the file as "index.html" in a folder on your computer. Open this folder and double-click the file that you have just saved. On most computers, this should open a web browser and show a blank (still!) page. If nothing opens after double-clicking, try right-clicking the file to choose a browser. Browsers that support p5.js are, for example, Firefox, Chrome, Safari, and Opera.

Let's try drawing something in p5.js. Use the previous template and enter the following code in the middle (you can replace "function setup ..." with the code). Then save and refresh the browser.

Draw an ellipse that follows the mouse position (P5.js)

```
// function definition
// (replace 'void' by 'function')
function setup() {
  // different function name (used to be 'size')
  createCanvas(640, 480);
}

function draw() {
  // slightly different variable name
  if (mouseIsPressed) {
    fill(0);
  } else {
    fill(255);
  }
  ellipse(mouseX, mouseY, 80, 80);
}
```

Once you move your mouse in the browser window, ellipses should be drawn. For comparison, this is the same sketch for Processing.

Draw an ellipse that follows the mouse position (Processing)

```
void setup() {
  size(640, 480);
}
void draw() {
  if (mousePressed) {
    fill(0);
  } else {
    fill(255);
  }
  ellipse(mouseX, mouseY, 80, 80);
}
```

Pretty similar, right? Let's move to the next part to see where the differences lie and how to move code from Processing to p5.js.

5.5.2 From Processing to p5.js

The basic question is how do you need to change the Processing code, so it can be run on the web with p5.js? We will touch upon four aspects in the following and refer to the browser environment by "Javascript" code. There is more complete information in the p5.js migration tutorial.[4]

Functions. Functions in Processing start with a data type (of what they return), or void. In JavaScript, we need to use the "function" keyword for that (see earlier).

Variables. Processing variables are declared using their data type such as int position, float rotationDegree, and boolean useSound. In JavaScript, variables are declared with the keyword "var" (or "let" in newest versions), no data type is necessary.

---

[4]https://github.com/processing/p5.js/wiki/Processing-transition

Mouse control. While we are using the mouse to control many sketches in Processing, the mobile environment often supports touch screens instead of a mouse. P5.js provides additional variables and functions to handle touch input and even multi-touch. In addition to mouseX and mouseY, you can use touchX and touchY as well as handlers for touch events.

Different function and variable names. In dealing with the browser environment, the p5.js developers had to implement some functions and global variables with different names. For example, the size function in Processing was renamed to "createCanvas" that works similarly. Another example is Processing's mousePressed variable that is called "mouseIsPressed" in p5.js.

Again, it is probably a good idea to refer to the information in the p5.js migration tutorial.[5]

5.5.3 Fine-tuning the presentation

When you open such a sketch in your browser, you will notice that it might not cover the entire browser width and height. P5.js provides two variables "displayWidth" and "displayHeight" to scale the web canvas to the full size of the browser window.

Scale the web canvas to the entire browser window

```
function setup() {
  // use variables to fill the entire browser canvas
  createCanvas(displayWidth, displayHeight);
}
```

---

[5]https://github.com/processing/p5.js/wiki/Processing-transition

There are further tweaks that you can apply to how the sketch is presented on desktop and mobile browsers. First, you should set the title of the sketch page to something recognizable as it will be displayed on tabs or in the header bar of the browser. The second change is about tuning the page display to the device. Mobile devices allow for switching off parts of the user interface elements or provide different scaling options than desktop browsers. The following example shows a good default setting for mobile experiences.

A template setup for mobile experiences

```
<html>
  <head>
NEW:
    <title>TITLE OF YOUR SKETCH</title>
    <meta name="viewport" content="minimal-ui, width=device-
    width, initial-scale=1, maximum-scale=1, user-
    scalable=no">

    // same as before ...
```

Finally, don't forget that mobile devices can be rotated. P5.js gives you a specific handler for this purpose,[6] which can be used to trigger a new layout or visual reset depending on your creative content.

---

[6]In P5.js, you can react on orientation changes, that is, when the user rotates their phone or tablet from landscape to portrait or back. This handler is called "deviceOrientation"; see https://p5js.org/reference/#/p5/deviceOrientation.

5.5.4 How to spot errors?

In Processing, errors are reported in red text in the console, the black area underneath the code. You have probably seen this once or twice (or a lot if you have been experimenting with code). A web browser, in which you would run your sketch with p5.js, does not show its "black area" by default. Still, it is there, just called "web developer" or "web console" (on Firefox), "developer tools" (on Chrome), or "developer console" (on Safari). Use a search engine to find out how to activate them for your operating system, browser, and browser version. This is usually quite easy if you know where to click.

This hidden view shows what is going on behind the scenes of a web page. You open this view on any website and analyze it, change it, or even experiment with its inner workings. For our purposes, we need to switch to the "console" view and check for errors (red) and warnings (yellow). If we print out information from our sketch via `print` or `console.log` on a website, this information will show up in the console usually as an "info" (white/blue) message.

Although JavaScript, the language we are using for programming with P5.js, is quite permissive in what it allows, it is good practice to structure code carefully, end lines with a semicolon, and write comments. Do yourself the favor and don't create code which embarrasses you in four months. Remember: if you can open the developer view, anyone can do that, also on your web page with your sketch. Your future self will thank you.

5.5.5 Deploying for mobile use

To deploy something online, you need a computer that is always running and connected, a server. You don't need to run this computer yourself (although you could do that from your home). Often there are free resources that give you a tiny slice of a server, which is sufficient for our purpose here. Note that you don't need to do this when programming for yourself. You only need a web server when you want your creation to be available for others around the clock.

Publishing on a web server is like accessing folder on a different computer and copying a few files to this folder. Once they have arrived, the server will literally "serve" them to any browser that requests them.

Given the minimal example for p5.js that we have used so far, you only need to upload a single file "index.html" to the web server. In case of larger projects with resource files and perhaps other libraries, you would need to make them available via the web server as well. As an example, we want to publish the minimal example on the web server behind "`https://codingart-book.com`" and upload the file "index.html" to the public folder "chapter5/firstexample". Then our sketch will be available at "`https://codingart-book.com/chapter5/firstexample`". We don't need to add "index.html" behind "firstexample" because "index.html" is the default file that the web server will serve when accessing a folder. This all reads perhaps difficult (all these files and folders), wait until you try it out. It's a piece of cake.

5.6 Summary

This chapter was about pushing your work from 80% to 100%. Sometimes, actually most of the time, moving from 80% to 100% may take even more work than going from 0% to 80%. Often an idea can be implemented and is running well on our computer, whereas when moving the work to another computer, or other devices (like projector or a mobile device), things can easily go wrong. Perhaps you didn't consider such problems during the process of coding the idea. That's fine and actually a good idea: let your creativity run free of constraints that only emerge during production. Once your project successfully reaches the production phase, some code might need to be rewritten according to the new conditions and contexts. But the concept is good and so is most of your existing code. Have confidence!

When we present our work in different contexts, this demands different levels of reliability than prototyping. We need to consider our idea, code, and production in a bigger picture and not as prototypes anymore. Compared to more traditional arts and design, we can expect more, a lot more, technical difficulties in creating with computation. Throughout the creation process, we need to find a balance between our ideas and the underlying technology. On the one hand, we guard and protect our fragile ideas and concepts; on the other hand, we cannot make the technology too complex and fragile. In this chapter, we explain the production step as a way to make your lives easier and to encourage boldness in taking creative steps. This step is the transition from nurturing to letting our creation blossom and shine.

Most examples, tricks, and hints contained in this chapter are the experiences and lessons learned from previous projects, workshops, and teaching Processing to students of all ages. This chapter covers by far not all topics we could think of, nor will the presented approaches be optimal in all cases. We believe that in design or art, there are no clear recipes or models. You need your own judgment and that comes with familiarity. That's all, but how will these steps work in practice? Read the coming chapter about the example MOUNTROTHKO. And what if something will not work? Come and visit the last part of this book! Now we continue with an example.

PART II

An example: MOUNTROTHKO

CHAPTER 6

Inspiration

The second part of this book deals with a larger example that applies many aspects of the first part of the book. For this part, we choose one of Yu's works, MOUNTROTHKO (2018). We want to emphasize that what we write about in this book is what we also practice: First, we show the conceptual and visual examples. Then, we walk through the four steps of the creative process in close relation to this example. You will recognize many aspects that we introduced in the previous chapters. We unfold the creative process of MOUNTROTHKO from the very beginning. Let's provide a bit more context before we get started.

MOUNTROTHKO was the second in a series of three projects created between early 2017 and August 2018. These three projects explored how to bring interactive technology into the three artists' works in different ways: notMONDRIAN was inspired by Piet Mondrian's work, MOUNTROTHKO by Mark Rothko's work, and THE FALSE MAGRITTE by René Magritte's work. MOUNTROTHKO was created from the end of 2017 until the beginning of 2018.

At the end, the whole work MOUNTROTHKO was presented as a collection of prints (Figure 6-1) and an interactive installation (Figure 6-2). The prints featured selected frames from three scenarios – "day," "noon," and "night." The interactive installation was set up in a 6.5 x 8 x 4m space with a 3 x 2.5m^2 projected surface and both motion and sound detection devices.

© Yu Zhang, Mathias Funk 2021
Y. Zhang and M. Funk, *Coding Art*, https://doi.org/10.1007/978-1-4842-6264-1_6

Yu took the lead as the artist in this project, and Mathias acted as the expert for the more complex programming structures, the animation, and, finally, an optimization step that allowed for real-time interaction. In the following, we describe this project and process from our team perspective ("we").

Figure 6-1. *Twelve selected frames from three scenarios of MOUNTROTHKO – "day," "noon," and "night"*

Figure 6-2. *The interactive installation was set up in a 6.5 x 8 x 4m³ space with a 3 x 2.5m² projected surface*

6.1 Context and starting point

In 2014, we visited a Rothko exhibition [9] at Gemeentemuseum[1] in Den Haag. Oliver Wick captured the visual experience of Rothko's work as "a sensation of standing on a threshold or of reaching out into space" [22]. Yu described this experience as "towering over me–big-scale paintings piled up chaotic but large and pure color blocks with smudged edge lines, yet not quite recognizable–couldn't simply be expressed by words like 'pleasant', 'entertaining', or 'joyful', or by even more abstract and open words like 'wonderful' or 'meaningful'. It was not a carnival of colors that cast an enjoyable mood over me. On the contrary, it would quickly pull me into a sensation of sentimental poetry." And further as "the feeling of being within the fold of language–positioned or placed by what we know: by standing in front of Rothko's work and staring at them for hours, the surrounding environment seemed to blur and to flow, not figuratively like a flowing river, more like flowing air with tiny and somber dust particle, invisible but somehow tactile, with the subtle sense of touch that every single dust particle was hitting the body and bouncing off again. The whole experience was becoming alive." For us, this first impression stays.

When we started MOUNTROTHKO as a project, it had been almost three years since we visited the Rothko exhibition. We felt inspired by Mark Rothko's work, because we were looking for a way of designing an artwork with "slow interaction," allowing for visitors to go deep into their own experiences. The concept of "slow interaction" is about slowly zooming into the artwork and gradually discovering a subtle feedback loop through interaction. By doing so, the designed experience can offer more options, perspectives, space, or time for visitors to understand and enjoy the artwork. Recalling our experiences of seeing Rothko's paintings at Den Haag, we wondered whether we could recreate Rothko's powerful concept of "accurate silence" [7] as an interactive, digital experience. For us, creating

---

[1]https://www.gemeentemuseum.nl/nl/tentoonstellingen/mark-rothko

MOUNTROTHKO was to deliver a moment of letting visitors discover aesthetics and elegance in static and dynamic visual layers and letting them immerse themselves in some form of flow state.

6.2 Concept and artwork

MOUNTROTHKO started with Rothko's "sense of depth in an otherwise abstract composition,"[2] going beyond the characteristic painting technique and style that Mark Rothko explored in the middle of the twentieth century. We observed that Rothko shaped simple visual elements into different layers. As a result, visitors' viewing experiences were complex because of the composition on the multiple layers where simple visuals were drawn and arranged. This principle came back in MOUNTROTHKO in the depth of visual elements and the almost undetectable dynamics when choosing not to interact and just observe.

Instead of quite literally reproducing the visual forms that Rothko used, we turned toward the natural motive of a formation of three mountains and set them at depth. On the one hand, "mountain" has a characteristic shape and almost visual gravity. On the other hand, distant mountains in Chinese traditional painting mean far, senseless, and silent but also the inexhaustible power to supply their surroundings. In MOUNTROTHKO, the mountain range was overshadowed by layers of fog that create further depth and, like the real weather phenomenon, could shift vertically and in translucency. The foreground was determined by particles that appeared and floated through the whole canvas in clouds and swirls which were not rendered as dots, but as complex composite shapes. Particles were rendered in several layers of depth, and they responded to wind and

---

[2]https://www.tate.org.uk/art/artworks/rothko-black-on-maroon-t01031

gravity dynamically, creating a rich foreground of the work. The particles somewhat extended the otherwise static artwork through time – even without visitors present.

As soon as visitors entered the installation space, the artwork would react to their movement and the ambient noise that was produced in the space. The first interactive part of this artwork was about shifting the visitor's viewpoint of the mountain range and also shifting the visitor's viewing time throughout the day. The horizontal position of the visitors in the exhibition space was tracked using a Kinect device. The artwork changed its visual composition and coloring rendering according to the visitor position in three scenarios – "day," "noon," and "night." The main idea was to explore the relationship between mountain formations, light, and particles from dynamic and static perspectives. Each scenario was special in the attention toward coloring, layering, and composition of forms. A second aspect of interaction was about the ambient sound in the installation space. We used the average loudness of sound or noise in the exhibition space to control horizontal movement of particles. With more sound volume, the particles floated more dynamically off and away from the surface of the digital canvas.

In both forms of interaction, we slowed down the time between visitor interaction and artwork response and also deliberately delayed the visual dynamics to strengthen the ambient feeling of the entire installation. The interaction emphasized the interplay of visitor, dynamic particles, and drawing the eye over a distant mountain range. Yet, through "slow interaction," visitors would subtly experience a finality that almost unravels in time.

CHAPTER 7

From idea to completion

Abstracting a bit from what can be seen and experienced, the entire concept of MOUNTROTHKO can also be divided into the static (central theme of mountain range), the dynamic (particles), the interactive (visitor movement tracking, sound processing, and corresponding visual behavior), and the parametric (complex color scheme depending on interaction and rendering settings). We will explain these different aspects of MOUNTROTHKO in this chapter.

When creating MOUNTROTHKO, we followed the steps from the first part of this book: idea to visuals, composition and structure, refinement and depth, and finally completion and production. Each step in the process is represented in the code of MOUNTROTHKO, and we pulled apart the code or zoom into specific sections to explain the different steps we take. We don't cover the entirety of the installation code.

7.1 Idea to visuals

This step is about starting with nothing but a thought, a feeling, an emotion, or a combination of these. It is something subtle and fragile that needs to slowly settle into a more concrete form and shape. We could have worked with sketches or text, but decided to express the initial ideas and

Y. Zhang and M. Funk, *Coding Art*, https://doi.org/10.1007/978-1-4842-6264-1_7

concepts with visual elements drawn on the Processing canvas. Ultimately, this shifted the direction toward a specific aesthetic that only creative coding can create. This way we found the core of the work, a "thing" that would stay with us till the end of the process as base expression of the idea in code.

In the process of settling an idea, everyone can take different approaches. Sketches, pictures, films, quick models, texts, and oral language are often used to clarify ideas after their initial inception. You could also try to express early ideas verbally to share them with others and receive feedback.

As we mentioned in the beginning, the experience of visiting Mark Rothko's exhibition is the inspiration for the MOUNTROTHKO project. We started by searching for additional inspiration, related concepts, and references to literature. We researched Rothko's work as a first step to better understand this artist and his work. This included his painting technique [16], biographical details [4] [5] [10] [17], and interviews and interpretations [11] from other art critics and researchers from both academic and practical perspectives [1] [2]. Through this process, Rothko's concept of "accurate silence" [7] emerged and was adopted as the original idea of this project: an experience of "accurate silence" through a dynamic, interactive artwork. More specifically, we wanted to create a dynamic frame of "a square that he conceived of as an environment" [19]. As a starting point, we defined the scope of MOUNTROTHKO as working with blurry, composed layers of visual elements that capture the interplay of form and color. Let's see how this worked out.

We did not begin the process with sketches on paper or graphics software. Instead, we sketched the initial ideas directly in code. We started with rectangles in different shades of a common base color which were randomly placed and varied in width and height. We used a mapping of the current horizontal coordinate of the mouse position to get a bit more control over the placement of the rectangles and their blending. Finally, we applied a BLUR filter to fuse the elements visually into the same plane (Figure 7-1).

Interactive, blurred rectangles in different shades of a common base color

```
rect(100, y, 200, 50 + mouseX);
// filled with randomly selected colors in the range
// flowing from yellow to red
fill(random(224, 250), random(150, 166), random(86, 135));
// strong blur filter at the end
filter(BLUR, 20);
```

This pattern was executed several times, for instance, with a for loop or the draw function, to obtain several layers (Figure 7-2). At later stages, we introduced transparency in the fill color (as a fourth parameter) and only varied the elements vertically (Figure 7-3), but let them span the entire width or height. We tried different color themes (yellow-gold-rust-carmine-red and Aegean-light blue-plum) and varied the order in which elements were painted by Processing. Some combinations were too obvious in their composition, but some already showed hints of complex color boundaries and interesting gradients. Within a few iterations, the visual element of the "mountain fog" was there (Figure 7-4)!

It might be surprising that the dominant visual element, the "mountain range," was not our starting point; it came much later. It emerged as a single component of the evolving fog that was singled out and then turned into a more iconic shape. We will come to that in the next section, after going through a few more iterations.

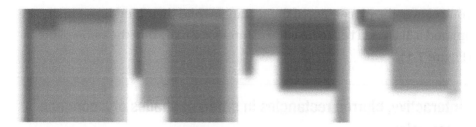

Figure 7-1. *Draw rectangles in different shades of a common base color and contain a blur filter*

Figure 7-2. *Use loop function to obtain several layers in visuals*

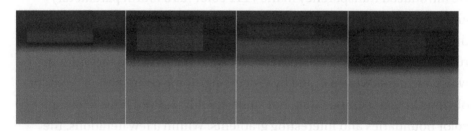

Figure 7-3. *Introduce transparency in the color to vary the elements vertically*

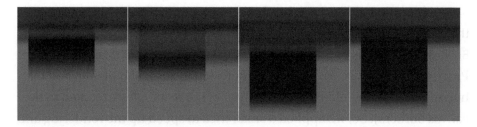

Figure 7-4. *Create "mountain fog" in the visuals by using both transparency and blur effects in motion*

7.2 Composition and structure

We explain in the first part that composition and structure can help refine the first achievements in code. Composition, in the sense of visual relationships between elements on a canvas, emerges when we code several visual elements and arrange them. It is a process of making connections between an idea and its expression in form and color. In MOUNTROTHKO, our process of coding the idea continued by taking over the visual elements from the previous step and combining them in different ways.

7.2.1 Composition: The fog

The first and only element that we have explored so far is the fog. A rectangle was used as the main visual element, and we repeated it to create layers of blurry shapes in variations of a common color. In the next iterations, we focused on the fog as a visual element descending from the upper border of the canvas and suspended over a strong unicolor background. By using different levels of blurring for each rectangle, we created an even stronger effect of color diffusion and tension between clarity and blur. To further explore different combinations, we introduced slow animations by means of controlling some parameters with the frameCount variable. We have used this earlier in the book to create simple animations.

At this point, we noticed that further progress was difficult, because the rendering of multiple large blurry shapes in Processing is slow. The BLUR filter needs to process every single pixel, and that takes time in Processing. However, we were only interested in vertical blurring, and the horizontal edges would be hidden anyway (the rectangles stretched to the canvas borders). So, we applied a small trick to speed up the rendering and allow for faster prototyping: we drew the blurry rectangles on a separate image canvas blur that is very narrow (only 5 pixels wide) and then stretched it while drawing with image to the full width of the canvas.

Speed optimization of the BLUR filter to allow for faster prototyping

```
// controlling variable
float y = 200;
// define the separate image canvas, very narrow
PGraphics blur = createGraphics(5, 1000);

// draw to the image canvas
blur.beginDraw();
blur.smooth();
blur.noStroke();
blur.fill(149, 51, 122, 200);
// use a variable y to animate this blurred shape
blur.rect(0, y, blur.width, y/2.);
// use variable y for blurring
blur.filter(BLUR, map(y, 0, height, 2, 50));
blur.endDraw();

// draw the image canvas stretched to the whole width
image(blur, 0, 0, width, 1000);
```

206

This trick creates nice smooth gradients and allows still for experimenting and tweaking the variables, without too much impact on the rendering speed. Each individual rectangle is filled with a specific transparent color, and the amount of blurring depends on the variable y.

After experimenting with this visual composition (Figure 7-5), the link to the idea became stronger. Still rooted in Rothko's concept of "accurate silence," at this step, the visuals connected with the kind of diffused and dead-silent artistic conception that we were after. Let's leave the fog for a while and move to the next visual layer: the mountain range.

7.2.2 Composition: Creating the mountains

In our concept, we needed a heavy element to counterbalance the lofty and blurry fog. So, the first step was to ideate possible shapes and to draw them right on the Processing canvas. One of the first ideas was to continue with rectangles, but to rotate them in place by 45 degrees. We started with one and quickly moved to a composition of three mountains drawn in different layers from back to front. The three mountains have the same original reference rectangle, and we varied their shape and color slightly according to the concept (depth displacement and depth of field).

Three mountains were coded in the order back to front, and we used again image canvases for the mountains (image instead of rect), so we could still use subtle gradients as coloring if necessary. We drew each mountain in rotated rectangular shape in its own transformation (using translate, rotate, and scale) (Figure 7-5).

Figure 7-5. *Create "mountain fog" as a visual element descending from the upper border of the canvas and suspended over a strong unicolor background*

Draw three mountains from back to front

```
// back-right mountain
pushMatrix();
translate(300, 0);
rotate(radians(45));
scale(2);
image(mountain3, 100, 0, width-400, 3000-400);
popMatrix();

// draw back-left mountain
pushMatrix();
translate(300, 0);
rotate(radians(45));
image(mountain2, 0, 160, 280, 1300);
popMatrix();

// draw front mountain
pushMatrix();
translate(width-300, 0);
rotate(radians(45));
image(mountain1, 0, 0, 3000, 3000-400);
popMatrix();
```

Tips   Note that the placement and sizing of elements in this work were often found by experimentation. Sometimes we cannot explain how we came across a combination of values that simply works. This is part of the reason why ideating in code should be fast and allow for frequent iterations: you want to try to do a lot of things and let "happy accidents" happen.

You can almost see the amount of experimenting when you look at the positioning of the different mountains. The mountain coloring was not shown in the code, but we tweaked this in the same way as the fog. The result was a multilayered composition that convinced us in terms of tension between colors, elements, and narrative. Still, there was a lot of work to be done.

7.2.3 Structure: Creating the particles

Learning from the Chinese performance technique in artistic expression where movement is used to serve as a foil to quietness on the stage,[1] we were thinking of introducing subtle movement. One of the first things that we tried was snow-like particles in the foreground. At first, they were randomly placed and flickered with every frame, so we turned toward more structure. We created a range of particle positions as PVector objects in code. We used the x and y coordinates of each PVector for the rendering location on the canvas and the z coordinate for the particle's speed in the vertical direction.

First of all, we created the data structure for the particle positions as an array of type PVector. We could start with an arbitrary number of particles and then see how their number of onscreen behavior fits the rest of the

---

[1]https://www.britannica.com/art/Chinese-performing-arts

scene. The positions were randomly initialized in the setup function, as shown in the previous examples, and we drew the particles in the draw function.

Draw the particles as a group in code

```
PVector[] positions = new PVector[140];
void setup() {
    // initialize other parts of sketch
    // ...
    for (int i = 0; i < 140; i++) {
        positions[i] = new PVector(random(100, width-350),
            random(100, 300),
            (i % 2 == 0 ? random(1, 3) : random(-3, -1)));
    }
}
void draw() {
    // draw other parts of sketch (mountains, fog) first
    // ...
    for (int i = 0; i < 140; i++) {
        // add upwards or downwards motion from z coordinate
        positions[i].y += positions[i].z;
        // reverse direction if particles move vertically out
        // of canvas
        if (positions[i].y > 600 || positions[i].y < 100) {
            positions[i].z *= -1;
        }

        pushMatrix();
        // translate to particle position
        translate(positions[i].x, positions[i].y);
```

```
// draw the particle image
image(light, 0, 0, 40, 45);
popMatrix();
    }
}
```

Just with this additional code, we can draw hundreds of particles (well, 140 here) in a specific area on the canvas and let them float around in a moderately random fashion (half of the particles float up, the other half down). The initial vertical motion direction is decided in the setup function with an expression that seems a bit difficult at first: (i % 2 == 0 ?random(1, 3):random(-3, -1)). Let's unpack this quickly. This expression creates a random value either between 1 and 3 or between -3 and -1 depending on the condition i % 2 == 0. This condition checks whether the modulo of 2 of i equals 0. As we have seen before, the modulo operation returns the division rest, and for "modulo 2," this is either 0 and 1. This means that with increasing value of i, the modulo of 2 will flip between 0 and 1 constantly. This is exactly what we need for letting the even particles float down (random(1, 3)) and the odd particles float up (-3, -1).

What is missing from the example is how we drew the shape of the individual particle in MOUNTROTHKO. We started with circular shapes and finally decided for something that resembles "tiny moons," each a short curve with a BLUR filter. We rendered this shape once into an image canvas and drew this canvas for every single particle at the respective position.

Draw the shape for a single particle

```
PGraphics light = createGraphics(200, 200);
light.beginDraw();
light.smooth();
light.noFill();
```

```
light.stroke(255);
light.strokeWeight(8);
light.arc(100, 100, 50, 50, HALF_PI, PI);
light.filter(BLUR, 5);
light.endDraw();
```

The result is yet another layer of a random structure of simple individual shapes that move slowly upward or downward until they exit the canvas and their vertical direction is reversed. By now, we have programmed several layers of different shapes and forms. Some layers are dynamic and move slowly (fog and particles), while other layers are static (the mountains).

What is important is that we programmed this in tiny steps that we tested in Processing until the overall composition fit our developing concept of MOUNTROTHKO.

7.3 Refinement and depth

When we wrote about refinement and depth in the first part of the book, we experienced it as a step of moving results of previous steps toward more satisfying expressions of the concept. Perhaps not so much toward what is perfect, but toward what we can be proud and confident of showing to others. Why not perfect? Because "perfect" is often at the end of a path from good to better that drags on for too long (if not forever). In the example MOUNTROTHKO, we were already quite happy with the overall composition and how different parts and layers of the work fit and play together. Still, we found plenty of aspects to refine and give extra depth.

The particles that we introduced at the end of the previous section needed a more organic feel and variation to not distract the viewer by their slight artificiality. Also, we wanted the work to respond to visitors through interaction and interactivity.

7.3.1 Refinement: Reshaping the particles

Before, the particles were drawn identically at different positions, moving at different speeds. Also their shape was relatively simple, which we changed first by drawing each particle as a composition of two arcs. This results in a birdlike shape when two arcs are placed directly next to each other. You see this shape in Figure 7-6 for the "noon" scenario of MOUNTROTHKO.

Figure 7-6. *Bird-like particles from the "noon" scenario of MOUNTROTHKO*

Use a composition of two arcs to reshape the particles

```
light.arc(170, 100, 100, 100, PI+QUARTER_PI, PI+HALF_PI);
light.arc(100, 100, 100, 100, PI+HALF_PI,
PI+HALF_PI+QUARTER_PI);
```

The next refinement is to pre-render five different versions of the particle with different size and transparency. But before we go into this, we have to show you how we create the particle positions now (slightly simplified):

Create the positions of the particles

PREVIOUS:

```
positions[i] = new PVector(random(100, width-350), random
    (100, 300),
    (i % 2 == 0 ? random(1, 3) : random(-3, -1)));
```

NOW:

```
positions[i] = new PVector(random(100, width-350), random
    (100, 300), random(1, 3));
```

We took the modulo check out and gave particles a random positive z coordinate. Just a small change that makes all particles slowly tumble downward. Back to the different versions of a particle: five different particle images are drawn on a transparent background (in the setup function) before the sketch starts running draw. We use a bit of BLUR in the five versions, which is also the reason why we need to pre-render them as images: drawing hundreds of particles and blurring them every frame would simply be too slow for a decent frame rate. When drawing the scene, every particle's position is checked for the z coordinate, and one of the five versions is chosen to be drawn. You can see this selection in the lower part of the next code snippet (Figure 7-7).

Figure 7-7. *Groups of particles from the "night" scenario of*
MOUNTROTHKO

Further control of the particle motion

```
// we use a different kind of for loop because it's shorter
for (PVector pos : positions) {
    // move the particle downwards
    pos.y += abs(pos.z);
    // reset location if the particle leaves the canvas
    if (pos.x > width)
      pos.x = -25;
    if (pos.x < -30)
      pos.x = width + 30;
    if (pos.y > height)
      pos.y = random(-1000, -30);

    // move to particle position
    pushMatrix();
    translate(pos.x, pos.y);
    // rotate based on vertical position
    rotate(radians(map(pos.y, 0, height, 0, 180)));
    // compute scaling depending on z coordinate
    float scaler = pos.z * 25;
```

```
    // rotate again (further) depending on scaler
    rotate(radians(map(scaler, 10, 35, 0, 360)));

    // select image to draw depending on z coordinate
    if (abs(pos.z) < 0.1)
        image(light5, 0, 0, 10 + scaler, 15 + scaler);
    else if (abs(pos.z) < 0.15)
        image(light4, 0, 0, 10 + scaler, 15 + scaler);
    else if (abs(pos.z) < 0.2)
        image(light3, 0, 0, 10 + scaler, 15 + scaler);
    else if (abs(pos.z) < 0.3)
        image(light2, 0, 0, 10 + scaler, 15 + scaler);
    else
        image(light1, 0, 0, 10 + scaler, 15 + scaler);
    popMatrix();
}
```

Tips   We use a new type of `for` loop here that goes through all `PVectors` in positions without the need for a counter variable `i`. This is slightly shorter and more concise.

In this piece of code, several things happen at the same time: First, we check whether a particle has left the visible canvas. In this case, we place it back at the opposite side. Then, the particles rotate according to their vertical position (see the first `rotate` call). This creates an effect of particles slowly tumbling down. We compute a value `scaler` that is used to rotate each particle and draw it in a different size with a different image (as explained earlier). Since all changes are depending on the z coordinate of the particle, the resulting composition looks quite natural with some sort

216

of "depth of field" effect. In summary, we added different particle images that were also rendered in different sizes and orientations depending on the particle's z coordinates (Figure 7-8).

Figure 7-8. *Twenty different compositions of visuals in one scene*

7.3.2 Depth: Adding interaction

The second step for the refinement was to add interaction to the sketch that allowed visitors to influence the dynamics of the artwork.

The first aspect of interaction was about the ambient sound that we could record with a connected microphone (most laptops and desktop computers support this out of the box). We wanted to use the sound level to influence the horizontal movement of the flowing particles: with more ambient sound, the particles would be "blown" faster off the canvas, and a quiet ambiance would let the particle tumble down undisturbed. In the following, we first explain how we record and process the sound and then how the sound volume influences the visuals.

We added the Minim library[2] that allows us to access the sound input of the system.

Import the Minim library to use audio input for interactivity

```
// audio library
import ddf.minim.*;

// audio input object
AudioInput in;
// control variable
float controlSnow = 0;

void setup() {
    // other setup code
    // ...
```

---

[2]The Minim library allows to use sound input and output, audio processing, and synthesis. It is available directly from the Processing library manager. The examples are recommended as they explain the basic functions well.

```
  // initialize sound
  Minim minim = new Minim(this);
  in = minim.getLineIn();
}
```

With this initialization, we could process the sound input in every frame (that is, call the function processSound from draw).

Process sound in every frame (called from `draw`)

```
void processSound() {
  // compute the overall volume of the sound
  float sum = 0;
  for (int i = 0; i < in.bufferSize() - 1; i++) {
    sum += abs(in.left.get(i));
  }
  // 1. add new values
  controlSnow += min(sum / 2., 5);
  // 2. constrain control
  controlSnow = min(controlSnow, 500);
  // 3. decrease over time
  controlSnow *= 0.99;
}
```

Tips   In signal processing, people would not add the absolute values, but instead the square (*sample²*), and then finally take the square root ($\sqrt{sum}$). We don't need this here, and our approach is a bit faster.

The processSound function computes the overall volume of the sound input by adding all absolute values of the left channel up. We have to use the abs function to avoid the different sound samples canceling each other out (e.g., a sample 0.4 and −0.3 would result in 0.1 as the mean, which would not give us a good approximation of the volume). From this volume, we compute a new value for our control variable controlSnow. This value is limited (hard limit of 500 and it gradually decreases by 100% - 99% = 1%) every frame.[3] We need to use this mechanism to ensure that the particles (1) respond quickly to changes in sound volume, (2) do not get unnaturally fast with very loud volume, and (3) always return to the baseline movement. These three points together set the boundaries for interaction and need to be tweaked depending on the installation context and aesthetics.

What is all this for? Good point, let's go into the visuals. We use the controlSnow variable in the dynamic drawing of the particles. Before, the particles were flowing straight from top to bottom and rotating on their way down. With controlSnow, we influence their horizontal position with the ambient sound. The following code shows how we add this to the particle drawing:

Ambient sound controls particles' horizontal positions

```
for (PVector pos : positions) {
    // move the particle downwards
    pos.y += abs(pos.z);

NEW:
    // move the particle with the wind (controlled by sound)
    float wind = constrain(map(controlSnow, 0, 500, -5, 5), 0, 5);
    pos.x += wind * abs(pos.z);
```

---

[3]We wrote earlier that the installation used the sound volume or average loudness. This example shows a different way to use the sound input volume.

When the room is quiet and the microphone does not record any sound, the variable controlFlow will have very low values which map to a minimal horizontal displacement. If there is sound like talking or noise in the room, the value of controlFlow raises. This higher value is mapped to a value slightly larger than zero that is added to the x coordinate of every particle. This results in the particle moving slightly to the right in every frame. From the visitor position, this looks like wind from the left that blows the particles to the right. As the sound in the room calms down, the value of controlFlow also decreases, and the horizontal displacement returns to zero: the scene is still again.

As you can imagine, there were a lot more subtle adjustments we applied throughout the project. Too many for you to go through. Let's move to the next and final stage.

7.4 Completion and production

When we arrived at the completion and production stage, we needed to consider how we wanted to exhibit the work. In the end, we went in two directions: an interactive installation and high-resolution printed artworks. For the first direction, we had to think about the exhibition space, setup conditions, and equipment facilities to adjust the code for its final presentation. And for the second direction, we needed to produce a few stills of the now interactive installation. They needed to be in a very high resolution for printing.

7.4.1 Completion: Installation in space

We produced MOUNTROTHKO in three scenarios – "day," "noon," and "night" – for a 6.5 x 8 x 4m³ space with a high ceiling and a white wall to project on (Figure 6-2). We used a high-resolution projector, and we placed a low bench in front of the projection surface. The bench was arranged with a bit of distance from the wall, and we could determine the visitor position (sitting on the bench or standing) using a Kinect device placed at the visitor's back. What was the Kinect or the visitor position for? We used the rough position to switch between the three different scenarios of MOUNTROTHKO ("day," "noon," and "night").

Before moving to the installation space, we prototyped this interaction in the simplest possible way: with the mouse position. We simulated the visitor position (left, center, and right) by different horizontal areas for the mouse. The mouse in the first third of the screen was mapped to the first scenario, the second third to the second scenario, and so forth. This is what we describe also as "backstaging" in the first part, a technique to prototype and make our life easier when dealing with unpredictable or complex input.

When we moved the installation to the installation space, we just had to calibrate the Kinect such that it would give us reliable position information that we could map in similar ways as the mouse position. This required a bit of experimenting with the Kinect position and direction. When trying this solution ourselves, we noticed that the scenarios would flicker and jump in some positions. The reason was that the position variable was directly controlled from the Kinect input and would sometimes jump very quickly between two values. We solved this problem by switching the position variable to a MemoryDot object that was updated from the Kinect. Remember that we introduced the MemoryDot in the first part as a way to smoothen the movement of particles and other objects on the canvas? In this case, we used the MemoryDot to transition smoothly between different input values.

7.4.2 Production in print

As a second direction, we wanted to produce beautiful high-quality prints of MOUNTROTHKO. To have a bit of choice, we rendered 37 high-resolution images from the code. As we explained earlier in Part 1,

Processing allows to save the rendered canvas in different image formats. In the final prints of MOUNTROTHKO, we wanted to get the resolution of images up to 9000 x 9000 pixels. Setting `size` to this larger canvas dimensions was not enough. Based on the redefined canvas, we needed to adjust the locations of the three mountains and randomly initialized locations of the particles (Figures 7-9, 7-10, and 7-11).

Next, we needed to find the right frames to render. Also this is described in more detail in Part 1 of the book. The last and the most important point was to fix the many variable parameters of the sketch as high-resolution images cannot be rendered in dynamics. We fixed the scenarios, colors, and the mouse position to static values. After all these preparations, we let the program run its course and render large images that were ready for printing. Actually, we did not need to post-process the rendered images. All colors and dimensions were perfect. We reached completion for this project!

7.5 Summary

In the past six years, we have been working together and going through different projects including MOUNTROTHKO. We notice that when using code as an expressive tool for art creation, in all the projects we have been doing, there is "something" in common. When we started this book, we define that this "something" in common is the series of steps we have taken in our projects and written in this book.

In this part, we use the project MOUNTROTHKO to illustrate the four creative coding steps which we explain in detail in the first part of this book. By using such an approach, we want to emphasize that these coding steps are derived from practice and stay relevant to practice.

We admit that the steps from the real practice are not as neatly, logically, and methodically arranged as what you read in this book. Most of the time, everything did not happen as a clear sequence of steps. For example, in MOUNTROTHKO, we have gone back and forth, repeatedly, between the first two steps many times. It took time to find the elements and movements which match the meaning we want to deliver through this artwork. In the third step, how to code the "slow" and "elegant" movement – like the snow falling in the wind – took us longer than expected to get exactly right. In the fourth step, trying to render the high-resolution static images from the interactive code became quite difficult because of the many color parameters.

The creative process as it happened in real practice is always much more chaotic and complex than the process described in this book. This is also part of the reason why we don't release the full code of MOUNTROTHKO. There are too many versions and variations of it, each a little messier than the other. The other reason has to do with artistic freedom and intellectual property, but that's a topic for another time.

Back to the process: especially when we are immersed in creation, we may involuntarily fall into a specific "rabbit hole" of something that appears to be urgent and important. This might happen to you as well. Not all creative flow is clearly rational, and you might even choose to forget for some time about all that process and focus on creative inspiration and the feeling of "flow." The steps described in this book are for us the core essence, the patterns that appear over the last years in practice (and teaching with Processing). And we hope this essence can help you not lose your direction and focus when coding your own creative work.

Figure 7-9. MOUNTROTHKO *in the scenario "day"*

Figure 7-10. *MOUNTROTHKO in the scenario "noon"*

Figure 7-11. *MOUNTROTHKO in the scenario "night"*

PART III

Coding practice

CHAPTER 8

Dealing with problems

If you are new to coding art, you see a promising, even exciting area with lots of wonderful things to explore. At the same time, you get the feeling that there is a lot of complexity and difficulty underneath all that wonder. Certainly not the most inviting view.

In the previous chapters, we have introduced you to Processing, and we have shown you plenty of examples that illustrate important concepts and serve as starting points for your own journey into creative coding. And still, you might wonder: how could I even do this myself? How could I start from a blank Processing sketch and achieve in code what I dreamt about last night (or during the morning shower). Good point.

This book follows a process from ideation to prototyping and finally production. While the last point comes late, we always stress that ideation and prototyping (making) are key and they happen in iterations. You have an idea, you express it in some form (code, comments, or even just text), and then you run it and go back to ideation. This process is what you should spend most of your time in. While we sketched this process as explicitly low threshold, you might get stuck here and there. This chapter is about getting "unstuck" – wherever you are in your process.

© Yu Zhang, Mathias Funk 2021
Y. Zhang and M. Funk, *Coding Art*, https://doi.org/10.1007/978-1-4842-6264-1_8

8.1 Helping yourself

The fastest way to get help is often helping yourself. It might not feel that way, but think about this: most of the information about what went wrong and that you need to eventually solve the problem is already in your head or on your computer. In 90% of cases, all you need is a pointer in specific direction or a pointer to look at the problem in a different way. That's it.

8.1.1 Error messages or nothing happens

Let's look at different problems and how to solve them step by step. The first type of problems is directly visible in Processing: error messages. In the same category are problems like Processing not running your sketch anymore or crashing suddenly. All of these problems occur suddenly, and they result from a recent change to the code. You might have typed a Processing keyword wrong (you get an error message) or forgot a semicolon (you get an error message). You might have copied and pasted some code from the Internet that simply does not match your previous code. And many other changes. Recognize the pattern?

The common pattern is that before the change, the sketch was working, but afterward, it does not work anymore. The first step that you can take is go back to the last version that worked fine. Do it. Immediately feels better, right?

With this small win in mind, carefully retrace the steps that you took forward. Which lines of code were changed? Did you make a typo somewhere? Did you insert code that has missing dependencies to variables or functions? It is important to work slowly from change to change and check in-between if the code still runs fine. Over time, you will get a feeling for risky changes and deficiencies of copied and pasted code.

8.1.2 Working with copy–paste

We use code that is written by others on a daily basis. Everything included Processing from the core; the libraries and the examples are open for you to get inspiration from. There is a lot more to find on the Internet, sometimes solving a very specific problem that only few people encounter, or sometimes providing something fundamental for a larger audience. In any case, using and reusing code from others is part of coding practice. This also means that we need to educate ourselves about when we are allowed to use such code from others and under which conditions. In almost all cases, it is a basic to give attribution to the creators of code that we use. That means we name them, thank them, and provide links for others to follow. This works both ways: as much as you save time and speed up your process, many creators of code love to hear about where their work is used, and they might even provide feedback or help you fix a problem. Again, avoid plagiarism and taking credit for the work of others at all costs!

Now to the more practical issues: When you copy code from a website or other resources and paste into your own code, you don't just introduce new code to your sketch. Attached to this new code are concepts, ideas, and approaches to achieve a particular solution. It is good to remember the context around the textual code that you copied. Why? Because this will influence how well the new code plays with existing code in your sketch.

For example, you have a variable counter in your existing Processing sketch that counts how many times the mouse was clicked, and the new code from a website coincidentally also has a variable counter to count every time that 100 items have been rendered. The mixed changes to counter from both old and new code might result in quite strange behavior of your sketch. Finding this problem can be hard, because counter looks like a familiar object (because you wrote it yourself).

? Think about this   We should say that `counter` is a bad variable name to start with: what is counted? How is it counted? What if you need to count another thing? `counter2`, seriously?

A safer way to work with copy and paste is to create a new function in your Processing sketch and to paste the new code into this function. Then, you try calling this function at an appropriate location in your own code and see if there are unforeseen problems. Next, you go through the new code and check for anything that might have an unwanted side effect.

Reminder   Looking at all this effort, we suggest being hesitant to copy and paste too much, especially when you don't fully understand the copied code. Also, be aware that working with larger pieces of code is always more difficult and slower than working with shorter code. So, pasting large pieces of code into your own program might be slower than first trying to understand the new code and only integrating a select piece.

A few examples of side effects are accessing and changing global variables; using canvas translation, rotation, and scaling; or changing styles like colors and strokes. For the first example, you need to really understand what is happening, the second can be mitigated by using `pushMatrix` and `popMatrix` around the new code, and the third can be helped by using `pushStyle` and `popStyle` around the new code. Once you make sure that there are no unwanted side effects, you can start trusting the new code and work with it in your next steps.

8.1.3 Reference documentation

In situations where your code runs, but does not deliver the expected results, it is a good idea to check the reference documentation of Processing (and any library that you might have used). The Processing reference documentation is available both on the Web and locally as part of your Processing installation (from the menu "Help"). It provides one or more examples of how to use a function in Processing, explanations of what the different parameters mean and what the expected output is, and often a more general explanation of the function.

Processing as a platform is built to support learning and getting to results fast. At the same time, the developers aim for a versatile toolkit of functions that can be used in many different contexts. An example is the fill function which sets the fill color for all the following statements that draw shapes or text. You can use this function with one (grayscale), two (grayscale with transparency), three (color), or four (color with transparency) parameters. The parameters result in different output also depending on the color mode (for instance, RGB or HSB). You see that this is a seemingly simple function that is very powerful in how it can be used. And it is not the only one in Processing. Compare the drawing of lines with line to curve. If you understand how you use line, would you have guessed how you would have to use curve?

The reference documentation is for exactly these purposes. It explains and unfolds the usage of core functionality. Even though we have used Processing for years, we went back to the Processing reference countless times for this book. No shame in that.

8.1.4 Searching for symptoms

When you have ruled out simple problems or you are stuck with something that just seems an impenetrable mess, it is time to turn to a search engine and feed it with search terms. This is how you can really speed up your discovery: Choose your search terms carefully. Think about how others would describe the symptoms of the problem that you have and include any error message that Processing gave you. It is important to note that you first need to search for symptoms and not the speculated root cause of your problem. Why? The symptoms are a fact, something that you have observed. The root cause is often a speculation and interpretation of the symptoms with a heavy dose of the same bias that brought you to the problem. If you get an error code or, in case of Processing (and Java), an explicit exception like `NullPointerException`, then include this in your search.

Once the search engine returns results, after filtering out the most obvious advertisement and scamming, you can do two things: check if there is a quick fix, or read more to better understand your problem. In many cases, there are quick fixes available that only take a few extra lines or configuration options to solve a nasty problem. Although quick fixes might be very convenient, don't spend too much time digging for a quick fix. Set yourself a time limit, and then continue the search to better understand your problem. Have other people found similar issues? If you seem to be the only one on the Internet having this problem, are your search terms correct? Could it be another, but related problem? Or have you seen this problem before? Quite often, we see patterns of problems appear more often.

For example, the aforementioned `NullPointerException` occurs frequently in Processing. It is a signal that Processing encountered an access to properties of an uninitialized object ("null pointer"). The following code shows this problem:

Code that triggers a `NullPointerException`

```
PVector position;
void setup() {
    size(400, 400);
}
```

```
void draw() {
    rect(position.x, position.y, 40, 40);
}
```

If you run the preceding code, you will immediately get a NullPointerException as an error message in Processing, highlighting the line `rect(position.x, position.y, 40, 40)`. Processing throws this error (at you) because `PVector position` is never assigned a real PVector object. The moment that Processing accesses the properties x and y of an unassigned object, it will fail and tell you that through an error message. What else would you expect a machine to do? You can easily help Processing here and fix the trouble by changing the first line.

Solve the problem by changing one line of code

```
PVector position = new PVector(100, 100);
```

In the end, you will spend a significant amount of time on trying to find out things that went wrong. But never think that this time is lost or wasted. Apart from solving your immediate blockage to creative momentum, you will learn valuable tricks or recognize patterns that help you avoid similar problems in the future. Solving problems is more learning than anything else.

8.2 Getting help from others

We have talked about helping yourself before, which is a fast, but passive way to interact with online resources. It consists of searching, browsing results, reading, following links and cues, and reading more. There are other ways to get help online: through communication with others, experts or not.

8.2.1 Finding help

For most programming languages, platforms, and systems, there are specialized online forums where anybody can join and ask for help. The more specific the forum is, the better chances are for finding people who are capable of helping (not necessarily experts), who are interested in problems like yours, and who are willing to help, dedicating their free time to you. Think about this: if you would post your problem on a general social networking site like Twitter or Facebook, would you really expect high-quality help? Only if you are connected directly to people that we described earlier (capable, interested, and willing). Most people on Twitter or Facebook would probably just like your post to "support" you, but ... well.

There are smaller subcommunities in social networks, but they are not always freely accessible and you cannot search for previous answers easily. Your chances grow when directly looking at the right forum or specialized discussion board. Two of these communities are stackoverflow.com[1] and openprocessing.org. (By the way, you are lucky if you are part of an educational institution, like a university. Your chances of getting help are very high if Processing or programming is part of the curriculum.)

8.2.2 Asking the right questions right

Now that you have found the right people (or the closest you could get), let's see how this could go wrong. Keeping seriously bad manners aside (you know what we mean: rude, tone-deaf, demanding, ignorant behavior), the number one mistake you can make on a forum is to barge in without having searched the historical forum posts for answers to

---

[1]`https://stackoverflow.com/`

your question. If you do that, you waste yours and others' time and definitely their goodwill. So, search before you ask, and mention that in your question, so people don't interpret your question as a duplicate of a previously answered question.

With this obstacle out of the way, the next challenge is to phrase your problem as a question worth answering. What is the clear sign that something went wrong, and how should the ideal outcome look like? What have you tried before? With which results? What is the environment that you tried (Processing version, computer type, operating system, memory, peripherals)? What is the output that you have observed? Did you log any data (e.g., with `println`)? Try not to write a very long problem description, but include everything that could be useful to helpers. Be aware that they don't know what you know. Things that are obvious to you might need several follow-up questions for them to understand.

8.2.3 Minimal working example

The easiest way for others to help you is to provide them with a minimal working example. This is an extract of your own code that is as small as possible and still can show the problem clearly. This is easier said than done. Copy your code into a new folder, and cut away all code that is or seems unrelated to the problem. Remove all unrelated dependencies, libraries, and resource. Continue until you have a few lines of code that can always demonstrate the problem when you or someone else runs them. At this point, you probably see the value of comments. Comments will also help others understand what you tried to do and which approaches did not work. It is best if you add instructions to the example, how to start it and how to reproduce the problem if interaction is necessary for that.

Probably you see the solution already; if not, the minimal working example can then be posted online together with your question. Hopefully, others will engage with the example code and help you by providing a solution approach. Be prepared for unfortunate case that it cannot be done (and you have to go back to the drawing board).

In any case, once you post your problem on a forum, try to be present, to respond timely to follow-up questions, and show your gratitude. When the problem is solved, say so. Many sites like StackOverflow have a button for marking an answer as correct. Sometimes you can "upvote" answers or comments. All these keep people engaged and create positive feedback loops around helping each other online. Maybe you can offer help, too?

Experience shows that in many cases, problems are solved by writing them down in a way that others can understand them and help. Through expressing your problem and packaging a minimal working example, you understand what actually cause the problem and can solve it yourself. This approach is sometimes called "rubber duck debugging": the act of solving your problem by verbally explaining it to a rubber duck (or another animal or a friend). Yes, we seriously suggest you talk to an object. Try that!

8.3 Working with experts

A different way of working is by involving experts in your creative process. These can be people that you find in your local community but also online. Unlike the often anonymous or pseudonymous helpers on online discussion boards, these are people that you trust and whose opinion you take seriously even if they contradict you or point you at your own mistakes. We give this topic a separate section to emphasize the distinction between the former helpers who are sporadically and infrequently pulled in – and true collaborators.

8.3.1 How can experts help you?

When engaging experts in a project, you need to have a clear idea about what skills or knowledge you need or which parts of your project you cannot do yourself. The latter part is an important consideration because for anything that you delegate in some way, you need to have a clear picture of its eventual outcome.

Experts that are involved in your project should be able to provide honest thoughts, ideas, and criticism – even beyond their area of expertise. The advice from experts often involves changing more than just a single part of the system, and you should expect and welcome such advice even though it might be tough to follow through.

You can take the divide-and-conquer approach and define areas in the project that can be tackled by an expert, ideally without interfering too much with the rest of the project. You can also work closer with the expert and engage in a more fluent process and conversation. It is worthwhile trying out different ways to collaborate. Go with what feels best. Be positive.

8.3.2 How to manage a project with experts?

Whoever you work with, agree with them beforehand how and how frequently you will interact, what your expectations are in terms of time investment, and what the project milestones are (if the project is that well defined). Think about how you will communicate and which kinds of responses others can expect from you. Finally, agree on compensation and attribution beforehand. Write it down and confirm it in emails. Think about why others would like to collaborate on the project with you. There needs to be something that you can offer, for instance, sharing the credits, a learning experience, your skills in another project, money, or even a party or dinner when everything is done. We have seen others struggle with their creative collaborations in the past, simply because they never thought about creating a rewarding process for their experts and helpers. In the end, they were doomed to an extreme fluctuation in experts and running out of options who to ask in the local community.

Experts tend to "know it better" and might not argue for labor-intensive solutions. In particular, technical experts might be more comfortable suggesting "smart" or automated solutions to a problem when the real solution is just more work (involving continuous quality control by the creative). For technical experts, working with creatives means to accept iterations and pushing for quality that is beyond the "natural" qualities of the expert domain. For example, the final stage of a project with a (technical) algorithm underneath needs several improvements in how the output is generated. These improvements have nothing really to do with improving the algorithm. But they still require plenty of changes to the algorithm.

? Think about this   This has to do with potentially different value systems: Which things do you value? How would an expert value things differently?

This situation can be difficult for an expert without the creative realizing this. The possible result is that both sides are not satisfied with the outcome: the creative, because their quality standards have not been met and the project feels unfinished, and the expert, because their intensive work in the end does not lead to better results and is not appreciated. When the final stage of the project becomes very intensive in terms of labor, time, and precision, it is good to realize that this is a normal thing to be expected. It requires good communication and constant exchange of thoughts to resolve this potential conflict. The creative as the project owner needs to lead this effort, balancing between pushing forward and keeping everyone on board.

Working with experts means sharing responsibilities for the success of the project and also sharing the attribution. Think of movie credits; they name sometimes hundreds of people for a variety of roles and obligations. Take this approach and give attribution to all people involved even though it is "your" project. A project is often only the starting point to a series of collaborations, which makes sense as you know each other better over time and can work more effectively. We found that the best collaborations take months or years to build, and then work is basically reading each other's minds. It happens surprisingly often, and when it does, it feels great.

CHAPTER 9

Learning path

When you have finished reading this book (the end is not that far away now), what's next for you? Hopefully, you have tried plenty of the examples and even went on and modified them on your own. Perhaps, you felt like going down a rabbit hole and exploring a Processing topic like curves (points on curves, Bezier curves, etc.) or 3D shaders (think of tiny "texture programs"). When we started this book, we wanted to create a reading-and-making experience that sporadically branches off in completely odd directions, driven by the reader's curiosity. Done that? Good!

In this chapter, we take a structured approach to what you could do next: from exploring Processing functions and libraries to connected technologies to realizing projects and also helping others. Let's go.

9.1 Going deeper into Processing

When working more and more with Processing, you will find that you can structure your own ways of using Processing in project which will benefit yourself and others.

Processing is a rich platform that offers a lot of opportunities for diving deep into subtopics. We mentioned two earlier (curves and 3D rendering), but there is more from static graphics (like our book cover) to generative art and very hip movie overlays; many things are possible. There are sites

© Yu Zhang, Mathias Funk 2021
Y. Zhang and M. Funk, *Coding Art*, https://doi.org/10.1007/978-1-4842-6264-1_9

like OpenProcessing.org[1] but also blogs and videos[2] online explaining new tricks and pushing the aesthetics of what can be done with Processing. You can visualize data with Processing and create games and collaborative applications. We have used Processing successfully for teaching how to design musical instruments and multi-modal experiences in the past.

9.1.1 Challenges to pick

In all this, it helps to have a concrete project that guides learning. A project grounds the steps forward and prevents you from getting lost in details at every turn of the road. The second important ingredient for a sustainable learning experience is to not aim too high. Pick your learning challenges such that the learning curve is not too steep and you can get into a positive flow. If you feel struggling constantly without any moment of success, disengage and make new plans.

When you start a project, be aware that it might be tempting to combine learning with a more serious output. Such a two-in-one nature can be valuable and motivation. However, be honest to yourself and others about your motivations to embark on the project journey. If it is a serious project with clear deliverables and deadlines, ensure that the priorities on delivering are clear; learning plays a smaller role here. For projects that are motivated by learning, manage expectations that others might have on the output. The desired outcomes of such projects are an enhanced skill set, new insights, and broader knowledge, not a very refined end result (although that might happen eventually as well).

---

[1]https://openprocessing.org
[2]https://processing.org/tutorials/

9.1.2 Building your own tool set

When working more and more with Processing, you will find that you use some tricks or patterns several times and they reappear from project to project. Instead of copying them, you could consider turning them into functions that are reusable in different situations. What is the learning point here? You go through a process of spotting a pattern, identifying its scope (where it applies and where not), isolating the pattern, and packaging it into a function that allows you to apply the pattern in various situations. Once you come across a situation where the pattern generally fits but does not apply 100%, you can introduce parameters to make the pattern more flexible.

As an example, let's say you have worked with motion and movement in the last seven projects. Throughout these projects, you designed with a specific way of motion easing (how visuals accelerate and slow down). You can refine this pattern in the subsequent projects toward a small library of moving things around with very specific qualities. This collection of functions can become your personal library, and it will allow you to work in the next projects much faster, because the movement part is taken care of.

We have done this once or twice in the book. For example, this is how we developed the MemoryDot class. You can take this principle further by bundling different functions and patterns into your own library. This will allow you to express creative ideas much faster and in more sophisticated ways than coding them from scratch. When you have compiled such a library bundle of functions, you can make this library available to all your Processing sketches by creating a Processing library. How? Find it out by starting a search with "Processing library how-to."[3]

---

[3]https://github.com/processing/processing/wiki/Library-Basics

9.1.3 Sharing your tool set with others

After using your own library a few times, perhaps you feel confident about its quality and want to share it with others who have helped you before or that you helped online. One way to share code openly online is using a website like GitHub, GitLab, or BitBucket. These sites allow for sharing code and have the proper online tools for doing this in a very structured way. While doing so, you will learn about version control systems (git and mercurial) and about writing documentation that helps others make good use of your code. There is a lot more to read and learn about these topics, and that's also why we only touch on it here briefly. It's your learning path, should you be interested in this direction.

9.2 Different technologies

Once you reach the limits of how you can express your ideas with Processing, it might be good to look at other technologies.

Still, we believe that starting a project with Processing has huge benefits in terms of quick creative "sketching" of computational ideas. In most cases, you can start like this and then change the underlying technology if that fits your output better.

9.2.1 Enhancing Processing

Processing is not only a versatile framework internally (with all its functions). With Processing, you can reach into a vast ecosystem of functions implemented in languages like Java, Groovy, Scala, Kotlin, and Clojure. Since over 20 years, talented people have built applications, frameworks, connectors, libraries, and examples in these languages that are in principle all available to you. A good starting point are the official and contributed Processing libraries that are linked on the Processing site and also available through the Processing library manager (in the menu "Sketch" ➤ "Install library..." ➤ "Add library..."). With just these Processing-specific libraries, you will have access to different modalities than standard peripheral input and visual output, to various ways to incorporate networking and connectivity in your work, or to advanced physical models for visualization and behavior simulation.

Coming back to our previous fictional example of a series of seven movement-related projects, you could use libraries to connect the movement on the screen to different input devices or to sound output. In the first two projects, you work with the mouse movement, but using the Kinect library, you use human skeleton tracking to drive the movement on screen with your arms and shoulders. Now, you can literally "push" the objects on the screen and connect aspects of human body control to visual display of movement. You can use your body as a mouse, if you will.

A good starting point here is the Processing libraries site to pick a few things that you install via the library manager. Then dive into the libraries' examples that are available from the Processing examples browser. Most libraries come with at least a few clear examples that demonstrate what you can do with the library and directly show you in code how.

9.2.2 Assessing feasibility

Another aspect of your learning path in Processing is about your growing ability to judge or assess what might or might not be feasible given the current available technology and skill set. This is conventionally the domain of experts that you possibly collaborate with: you describe what you want to do, and experts assess whether this is possible and under which conditions. Only then the team would move forward with the project. Creative sketching with Processing essentially challenges this clear division of roles and aims at empowering you, the creative, to self-assess concepts and project it into the future based on tools and technology.

How does one acquire this skill? It would be too simple to answer "experience, years of experience." Assessing the feasibility of an approach can be understood as the walk down a mental path from idea and concept to a working prototype. It means (mentally) visualizing step by step how every stage of a work builds on a previous stage and that there is no magic involved in any part of the path. If things get blurry or involve some sort of technical magic, stop. Think back about what you have read in this book so far. Wouldn't you be able to judge that working with a particle cloud or with texture is generally feasible? Of course you would (if not, check out Part 1 again). Would it be possible to render the title of this book using a particle cloud? Let's think: particle cloud (done, check), text rendering (works, check), and the combination of text position lookup and particle movement? Seems tricky, but not impossible.

9.2.3 Moving away from Processing

In specific cases, Processing might not be a good choice to further prototype and develop a final work. Processing is based on the Java language and its runtime engine. This layer allows to run Processing sketches without any modification on different platforms and operating systems. However, this takes a toll: speed. The Java runtime engine is an intermediate layer between the Processing sketch and the operating system and the hardware. That means things can be a little slower, especially things that involve hundreds or thousands of computing steps – like rendering in 3D or rendering "many things."

There are other technologies that don't have this bottleneck, but might be harder to work with in the beginning. One example is openFrameworks,[4] which is a platform similar to Processing (functions are even named similarly), however based on a different programming

---

[4]https://openframeworks.cc/

language: C++. On the one hand, this requires different ways to code and develop creative work and, on the other hand, allows for higher execution speed.

Other examples are PureData[5] or Max[6] which are visual, flow-based programming languages, each with their own runtime environment. They were designed to help develop creative work that is based on signals, sound, and video streams. These languages follow the idea of providing building blocks that are highly optimized for speed and allow the user to connect them in very flexible ways. The connections just tell the framework how the data should flow; the rest is done by the internal building blocks, which results in a very different creative flow than with Processing.

It is a very worthwhile direction to explore the computational world around and beyond Processing. You will see that different technologies place different emphasis on core principles. Some are focused on learning and sketching, some are focused on working with data or audio signals, and some emphasize connections with other technologies. The more you experience, the better you will be able to make a choice when the next project comes along or inspiration strikes, which brings us back to the creative process of coding art.

---

[5]https://puredata.info/
[6]https://cycling74.com/

CHAPTER 10

Creative processes

In this chapter, we look at creative processes that involve computing and data as material. We intentionally put this chapter in the last part of this book, also as a reflective perspective on what we wrote earlier. We emphasized making over thinking in the first two parts; now it's finally time to explore the framing of this book. We start with the ideation and look at two different approaches before proceeding with abstraction layers and ways to shift technical perspectives within our work.

10.1 Two types of ideation

In the following, we will intentionally polarize a bit and try to distinguish two different approaches to ideation. We know that this distinction is a bit extreme and does not happen exactly as described in real life. Instead, most creatives use a mix of both approaches, perhaps in iteration, to come to meaningful results.

Nevertheless, let's have a look. What we see when creative work involves technology are basically two different approaches to ideation: concept based and material based. The former asks: given the concept in mind, how can I creatively use the material at hand? The latter asks: given my creative exploration of the material at hand, which concept could meaningfully build on it? We will describe in the following how this unfolds when working with Processing.

© Yu Zhang, Mathias Funk 2021
Y. Zhang and M. Funk, *Coding Art*, https://doi.org/10.1007/978-1-4842-6264-1_10

253

10.1.1 Concept-based ideation

In this approach, the creative work starts conceptually, probably long before Processing is touched. The core challenge is that there is an abstract idea in your mind and you need a starting point for Processing to ideate through coding. This means often that you know how the idea could possibly unfold and how this would look, sound, or feel.

A common strategy is searching for examples, for other people's work that seeds the coding process. You might find examples online directly, or through interaction with others, and start changing the example code toward your idea. A visual search starts with a description of the visual idea. Find the right words that concretely describe your idea visually. There are online resources you can start with, for example, Google Images, OpenProcessing.org, or even the Processing reference manual. These sources will deliver different kinds of results: a generic image search engine will likely produce very diverse results that are often not produced with Processing, so they come without source code. OpenProcessing.org and similar sites, as well as the Processing reference pages, contain the source code. As we have pointed out before, working with other creatives' code can be challenging. It requires understanding how their code works, but most of the time, you can start with small changes and develop your understanding of the code by seeing how it reacts to your changes.

10.1.2 Material-based ideation

Another approach is to start from the material, in this case, coding with Processing. Unlike physical materials like paper, glass, wood, and clay that are used in traditional fine arts and design, computation and programming of computational machines (computers) represent a new type of creative material. Material-based ideation is about exploring what this material can do, how it responds to our interactions, and how it pushes back when we poke it. The questions that we ask could be: "What can this technology do for us?" "How does it do this?" And "where are the limitations and how to cross boundaries with the material?"

There might be more technical questions, but it is worthwhile to stay focused on the high-level challenges. Only after several experiments with the material, the creative starts to gradually shift toward a more concrete theme or concept of their work. Given the technological material, what is a meaningful concept that connects to it at which level? How can the concept then build on the technology through several iterations? How might the concept demand something different or more from the material than previously (thought) possible?

These two strategies have different focus points. While the concept-based approach views technological material as a means to communicate a concept, the second material-based approach looks at a material differently and treats the concept as a way to frame and elevate the material that is at the core of the creative work. As we write in the beginning of this section, the division is not that explicit in real life. Creative work is by definition flexible in choosing and switching approaches and methods. Follow your heart.

10.2 Using abstraction layers

When we show you examples of code, these examples are always condensed, so they (mostly) fit within a page and compress a few learning points that are unfolded in the text. There is another way to look at the examples: by identifying and differentiating layers or components in every example.

We will do this here as we talk about their integration in creative processes in several steps that are linked to different iterations. The iterations mean that we will create a connection between layers and iterate several times before moving on. We start with the simple behavior–output combination that we showed at the beginning of Part 1.

10.2.1 First loop: Behavior to output

The first loop is about understanding that a sketch has behavior and from that generates an output on the screen, even though there is no interaction yet. We describe this loop mainly in the first part of this book, where we aim to translate ideas into visual elements and transform their presentation in the output. Let's look at an example.

Draw a white circle that rotates around the center of the canvas

```
void setup() {
  size(400, 400);
}
void draw() {
  background(0);
  translate(width/2, height/2);
  rotate(radians(frameCount));
  ellipse(20, 20, 20, 20);
}
```

This example shows a white circle that rotates around the center of the canvas. The code is quite simple and consists purely of drawing or positioning commands. Every frame we erase the background, position with canvas with translate and rotate, and finally draw the circle with ellipse. The positioning is at a fixed point in the center of the canvas, and the rotation depends on the frameCount. We have seen this pattern before in the book.

This is simple behavior that generates simple output. We might want to iterate on the looks of the visual elements, for example, the color or the rotation distance from the center. Such an iteration results in different programmed behavior and output, but we do not move beyond the main ingredients, behavior and output. To do that, we need data.

10.2.2 Second loop: Adding data

A bit further in the book, still in the first part, we introduce how data and data structures help in creating more complex behavior and output, for instance, when they involve many things or changes that progress over several frames. Before, we have used the draw loop as the only way to draw, and one iteration of this loop does not connect to the previous or next iteration – it stands for itself.

Data changes this as we can store data as a memory of what happens in an iteration and proceed to use this memory in the next iteration. Let's try this with the preceding example.

Introduce the position variable in the previous example

```
PVector position = new PVector();
void setup() {
  size(400, 400);
}
void draw() {
  // data
  position.x = width/2 + cos(radians(frameCount))
  * 20;
  position.y = height/2 + sin(radians(frameCount))
  * 20;
  // drawing output based on data
  background(0);
  ellipse(position.x, position.y, 20, 20);
}
```

Comparing this to the previous sketch, we see the same behavior and output here: a white circle moving around the center of the canvas. The code looks different though. In this example, we introduce data (the position variable), and in the draw function, we first change the data and then draw it. Essentially, we have separated the data and the drawing. We can now change the data independent of the drawing part, for instance, by adding interaction that influences the data.

10.2.3 Third loop: Adding input and interaction

When we add input, we create also behavior that deals with unpredictable, but not unexpected data. What does that mean? Interaction input cannot be predicted really, whether a user moves the mouse 20 or 34 pixels to the right within 2.3 or rather 5.4 seconds. That does not mean that we cannot deal with this input data. We just have to make our data structures and sketch behavior more robust to deal with user input. In that moment, we have created a better sketch that will likely show richer output than the first two versions, simply because it works with more diverse input data. In the next example, we just change the data part.

Let circle rotate around the mouse pointer

```
// data
position.x = mouseX + cos(radians(frameCount)) * 20;
position.y = mouseY + sin(radians(frameCount)) * 20;
```

First, we set the positioning around the mouse pointer, by using the mouseX and mouseY variables to control the position of the rotation center. We see now that the rotating circle can change its position based on the rotation center controlled by the mouse. One step further, we introduce two new variables that control the rotation speed and distance.

Add variables to control rotation speed and distance

```
// data
float speed = 10;
float distance = 20;
position.x = mouseX + cos(radians(frameCount) * speed) *
distance;
position.y = mouseY + sin(radians(frameCount) * speed) *
distance;
```

Note that nothing changes in the behavior yet, but we prepare for making both speed and distance change according to the speed of the mouse. We compute the distance of the current mouse position to the previous mouse position (pmouseX and pmouseY) with the dist function. This distance is now used in the speed and distance variables.

Use the distance between current and previous mouse position

```
// data
float energy = dist(mouseX, mouseY, pmouseX, pmouseY);
float speed = map(energy, 0, 30, 4, 0.5);
float distance = map(energy, 0, 400, 30, 100);
position.x = mouseX + cos(radians(frameCount) * speed) *
distance;
position.y = mouseY + sin(radians(frameCount) * speed) *
distance;
```

Unfortunately, the effect is not very clear. As we move the mouse fast, something seems to happen, but when we slow down to see closely, the effect disappears. The "energy" of the mouse is gone too fast to actually see the effect well. What we need is an extra piece of data that somehow conserves the energy and that releases the energy slowly so we can observe the effect. Let's make energy a global variable, and let it store the energy and slowly decrease down to zero.

Store distance in an " energy " variable

```
PVector position = new PVector();
float energy = 0;
void setup() {
  size(400, 400);
  stroke(200);
}
void draw() {
  // data
  // add distance to energy
  energy = energy + dist(mouseX, mouseY, pmouseX, pmouseY);
  // reduce energy every frame by 2% (100%-98%)
  energy = energy * 0.98;
  float speed = map(energy, 0, 30, 4, 0.5);
  float distance = map(energy, 0, 400, 30, 100);
  position.x = mouseX + cos(radians(frameCount) * speed) *
  distance;
  position.y = mouseY + sin(radians(frameCount) * speed) *
  distance;
  // drawing output based on data
  background(0);
  ellipse(position.x, position.y, 20, 20);
```

```
// add two lines
line(position.x, position.y, 0, height/2);
line(position.x, position.y, width, height/2);
}
```

We store now the energy of the mouse movement and still reduce it by multiplying the value of energy with 0.98. These two lines ensure that the energy from the mouse movement is stored and that the storage slowly releases. Now the effect should be clearer. To visualize the movement better, we also add two lines at the end of draw that connect to the left and right sides of the canvas.

Still, we might not be fully happy with the distances and speed. We can add "backstaging" to fix that.

10.2.4 Fourth loop: Adding a backstage

When we add a backstage, we implement a counterbalance to the user or visitor interaction input. This counterbalance allows the creative to steer the behavior on top of the input data and allow for second-order aesthetics that play, reshape, or negate the input data. Backstaging is not only a means to fix, debug, or maintain an experience, it's also a creative technique in its own right.

To add backstaging to the current example, we just need to run it in Tweak mode, which allows us to adjust any value in the sketch. Why is it again called "backstaging"? Because the Tweak mode works independent from the primary interaction with the mouse and acts directly on the code. While it might feel also as interaction, there is an important difference here: normal interaction does not change how the code works fundamentally; it does not have lasting changes. The Tweak mode and other backstaging aim to have a lasting effect on the experience and the behavior of the sketch.

10.2.5 Creative processes with layers

Throughout this section, we have looked at an evolving example through the lens of abstraction layers and loops between them. We start with a loop between the layers of behavior and output and then add data. By separating these layers to some extent in the code, we are able to make changes to one layer without changing the others. This leads to a more structured way of working with code. Ideally, we make a change and then run the code again to see the change reflected in the output. If we change the data and leave the behavior the same, what will happen to the output? If we change the data through interaction and leave the behavior the same, what will happen to the output and can we still influence it with backstaging?

The draw function is the central point of many Processing sketches. This is where the animation action happens. It is tempting to combine all drawing behavior tightly with data and interaction. We have done this in almost all examples in the book to ensure that the code is concise and fits the book format. As your skills and sketches develop, you might appreciate a different way of organizing code in draw. Instead of tightly interweaving input, data, behavior, and output, try to separate them in draw and in other functions.

Organize code in draw

```
void draw() {
  // input (interaction, network, etc.)

  // data

  // behavior

  // output
}
```

At first, you write code to deal with the input, for example, reading the mouse position or acquiring sensor data. The next step is to modify data structures according to the input. This data drives the behavior of the sketch, which then results in output.

Conclusion

This book has come to an end. We have written elaborately about how to approach "coding art" in several steps that move along a creative process. We wrote this book quite differently from conventional programming books and also quite differently from publications on art and on creative processes. In this book, we combine these two perspectives (code and the creative process), because we believe in their cohesion and mutual enrichment.

Over the years, we have seen countless young creatives struggle with the formalism of code that is introduced "just because." The rigid structure of a computing curriculum that follows the logic of the machine and not the human and creative needs is not helpful to our deeper understanding of what technology can be. At the same time, we have seen people struggle with their creative processes once technology is involved; they lack starting points, confidence in building achievements, and access to richer concepts than the absolute basics. This is why this book starts and ends with creative processes and tempers the role of code by curiosity and creative pull. Why would you need to know about functions, recursion, and classes if not clearly motivated by what they add to your creative practice?

In the introduction, we direct the book's message to three main audiences: creatives, educators, and technologists. We hope that you found yourself, even if you don't see yourself as part of these groups. We did write this book for you!

Thank you for staying with us until the end. We wish you lots of exciting moments and beautiful experiences creating and pushing your limits with code.

Goodbye for now!

© Yu Zhang, Mathias Funk 2021
Y. Zhang and M. Funk, *Coding Art*, https://doi.org/10.1007/978-1-4842-6264-1

Epilogue

Before we had the fully formed plan of writing a book for creatives, educators, and technologists, we wanted to write about coding in art and design since early 2017. For me, the intention of writing this book became stronger since I finished my PhD, and expression through code became more and more important in my work. Reflecting on my own learning experiences in the years prior, I realized that to produce and ensure the stability of both the code and the production for an interactive installation are far more important than just having an idea in mind. In addition, there are so many other key points when going deeper into practice: working with experts, asking for help, producing the same installation with its technology in different exhibition spaces, and knowing what to stick to in the process and when to change course.

Writing about all these realizations, turning them into clear lessons and steps, was not easy and also motivated by own experience of starting to teach interaction design in a traditional design faculty. I found that due to the lack of process and training in coding and technology, my students struggled with imagining what interaction could be and how experience could be designed. Many students gave up after just taking a few steps. For them, learning to use code to create is very different compared to other types of creative tools. They needed a bit of a change of mind, a better approach, and different inspiration. When writing this book, we started with the creative process and creatives' needs, instead of following technology. And it works.

—Yu

Y. Zhang and M. Funk, *Coding Art*, https://doi.org/10.1007/978-1-4842-6264-1

Now that you have reached the end of the book, let me explain a few thoughts that brought me to writing this book with Yu. When I started to teach Processing in a course called "Creative Programming" and also later in several workshops, I was amazed by how fast students and workshop participants could achieve interesting, funny, ridiculous, or beautiful results with Processing. This platform helped them type along, try out variations of what I showed them, and find their own creative path. Still, I felt limited by how "programming" with Processing was taught. In many cases, there are very approachable starting points online like "draw a green rectangle!" or "do this and – wow – look what happened!", but soon after, the topics would resemble a long list of functions or traditional programming topics. Computational creativity and creative processes deserve different attention, even though we are talking about code.

One of the best experiences I had teaching Processing was the most ad hoc one in March 2016. I opened Processing and started typing and talking out loud. My laptop screen was mirrored on the wall. The participants of this short workshop watched me type on the screen, making the occasional mistake or typo, which I explained and corrected. They just typed along bringing in their own variations of what I showed on my screen. Over the next two hours, we touched on most shapes and some animation options. No slides, bullets, and formulas were necessary for getting everyone up to speed. After this workshop, the participants would form teams and continue to work out quite complex sketches and prototypes.

A second thought about teaching in a design faculty: I'm sometimes puzzled by how little courses prepare for the actual difficulties of working with code and the complexity that develops after the first few steps. Looking at example code and purposeless tweaking of existing examples from the Web seems easy and straightforward, but what if one has a concept in mind and needs to code it? What if there is nothing online resembling your goal in any way? What if you are stuck after tweaking for hours? When encountering these and other problems, I could help given my background and experience. More often than not, the steps toward getting "unstuck" were simple and almost followed a recipe. But nobody thought about teaching this.

For quite some time, I wondered how to bring this experience into a more shareable format and, at the same time, extend the topics while keeping closely in touch with creative processes. This book is the solution, and we structured the book not along programming topics, but instead developed it by following our own processes and experiences. In this sense, we move fast through the basics explaining relationships and examples, but we leave out a lot of information that you, the reader, can find neatly organized in the Processing reference.

We want to inspire creative flow and wrote the book like that – a flow from the initial inspiration and ideas toward more and more developed structures and complexity that inevitably enters the picture when inspiration strikes and materializes designs and artworks.

Working with Yu on this book was a special experience, shifting perspectives many times, working out ideas and examples in detail, and rewriting most of the book. I hope you will have as much fun as we had (a lot!) when discussing and writing this book for you.

—Mathias

References

1. Star Arts. Mark Rothko complete documentaire. https://www.youtube.com/watch?v=e135VhG4IgA, 2016. Accessed: 2018-12-14.

2. ARTtube. Mark Rothko. https://www.youtube.com/watch?v=Cosm67tJ5VY, 2014. Accessed: 2018-12-14.

3. Stefania Bocconi, Augusto Chioccariello, Giuliana Dettori, Anusca Ferrari, Katja Engelhardt, P Kampylis, and Y Punie. Developing computational thinking in compulsory education. European Commission, JRC Science for Policy Report, 2016.

4. James EB Breslin. Mark Rothko: a biography. University of Chicago Press, 2012.

5. Annie Cohen-Solal. Mark Rothko: Toward the Light in the Chapel. Yale University Press, 2015.

6. Jan Cuny, Larry Snyder, and Jeannette M Wing. Demystifying computational thinking for non-computer scientists. Unpublished manuscript in progress, referenced in https://www.cs.cmu.edu/~CompThink/resources/TheLinkWing.pdf, 2010.

7. Linda DeBerry. Silence is so accurate: Thinking about Mark Rothko. https://crystalbridges.org/blog/silence-accurate-thinking-mark-rothko/, 2014. Accessed: 2018-10-14.

© Yu Zhang, Mathias Funk 2021
Y. Zhang and M. Funk, *Coding Art*, https://doi.org/10.1007/978-1-4842-6264-1

8. Shelley Esaak. What is the definition of texture in art? https://www.thoughtco.com/definition-of-texture-in-art-182468, 2018. Accessed: 2019-02-01.

9. Gemeentemuseum. Mark Rothko. https://www.gemeentemuseum.nl/en/exhibitions/mark-rothko?gclid=CJ6zxNys6MICFUsJwwod5KIAtw, 2014. Accessed: 2018-10-14.

10. Grace Glueck. A newish biography of Mark Rothko. https://lareviewofbooks.org/article/a-newish-biography-of-mark-rothko/!, 2015. Accessed: 2018-12-14.

11. Alexxa Gotthardt. Mark Rothko on how to be an artist. https://www.artsy.net/article/artsy-editorial-mark-rothko-artist, 2018. Accessed: 2018-12-14.

12. Milton D Heifetz. The aesthetic principle. Art Journal, 25(4):372–375, 1966.

13. Lucy Lamp. Design in art: Scale and proportion. https://www.sophia.org/tutorials/design-in-art-scale-and-proportion, 2013. Accessed: 2019-01-30.

14. Lisa Marder. What does the term 'form' mean in relation to art? https://www.thoughtco.com/definition-of-form-in-art-182437, 2018. Accessed: 2019-02-01.

15. Piet Mondrian. New York City. https://www.wikiart.org/en/piet-mondrian/new-york-city-i-1942, 1942. Accessed: 2019-01-30.

16. The Museum of Modern Art. The painting techniques of Mark Rothko. https://www.khanacademy.org/humanities/art-1010/abstract-exp-nyschool/abstract-expressionism/v/moma-painting-technique-rothko, 1998. Accessed: 2018-12-14.

17. Mark Rothko. The artist's reality: Philosophies of art. Yale University Press, 2006.

18. Dustin Stokes. Aesthetics and cognitive science. Philosophy Compass, 4(5):715–733, 2009.

19. Tate.org.uk. Restoring Rothko. https://www.khanacademy.org/humanities/art-1010/abstract-exp-nyschool/abstract-expressionism/v/restoring-rothko, 1998. Accessed: 2018-12-14.

20. Charles Albert Tijus. Cognitive processes in artistic creation: Toward the realization of a creative machine. Leonardo, pages 167–172, 1988.

21. Michael Gr Voskoglou and Sheryl Buckley. Problem solving and computational thinking in a learning environment. arXiv preprint arXiv:1212.0750, 2012.

22. Oliver Wick. Mark Rothko. A consummated experience between picture and onlooker. Fondation Beyeler (Hrsg.): Mark Rothko, Kat.-Ausst. Fondation Beyeler Riehen Feb–April, pages 23–34, 2001.

Index

A

Abstract geometrical
      painting, 9, 10
Animation
  basics
    draw function, 42
    functions, 42
    general structure, 41
    Processing, 42
    setup function, 42
  ellipses, 51
  mouse movement/click, 51
  mousePressed
    function, 52, 53
  movement
    calculations, 44
    frameCount, 43
    move/rotate, 44
    small rectangle, 43
  rhythm motion
    abs function, 47
    frameCount, 46
    horizontal movement, 47
    modulo operator, 49, 50
    sin function, 46, 47

B

Backstage
  keyboard, 165–168
  Tweak mode, 162, 163
  variables, 163–165
BLUR filter, 203, 206

C

Canvas secrets
  resetting/restoring
    defaults, 35
    popMatrix, 35
    pushMatrix, 35
    resetMatrix, 34
    selectively roll back, 35, 36
  rotation/translation
    black rectangle, 36–40
  scaling visual elements
    scale function, 32, 33
    values, 32
Coding art
  computation/code, 2
  cooperative skills, 6
  creatives, 6–8